The Promising Few

Table of Contents

Introduction 4
Act I 11
   Scene I. Hazelton 12
   Scene II. Candidacy Stage 46
   Scene III. Forbidden Temple 55
   Scene IV. Candidacy Stage 72
   Scene V. Lake of Love 84
   Scene VI. Judgement Day Stage 92
   Scene VII. Voting Stage 133
Act II 167
   Scene I. The Fruitful Forest 168
   Scene II. City of Hahm 177
   Scene III. Swallowing Swamp 258
   Scene IV. Hot Springs 298
   Scene V. Zaguah's Lair 344
Act III 403
   Scene I. Sucrex City 404
   Scene II. Mount Paramountain 420
   Scene III. The Sucrex Cave 429
   Scene IV. Mount Paramount 465
   Scene V. Hazelton 477

Introduction

Narrator:

Four men of bravery, greed, kindness, and strength

All seek the throne of Hazelton.

These four men are no strangers to another,

They are cut from the womb of the same mother.

This poor town is small yet simple,

And these four men serve the people.

They were born with a greater advantage,

And their skills left them with a town to manage.

They are well known across Hazelton.

Loved by many, spited by none.

The eldest son of Love and Creed

Is no other than The Handsome Greed.

He has lots of money and lots of ladies,

And without knowledge, lots of babies.

But what makes Greed ever so greedy,

Is his smartness, his only ability.

He's well with maths; he created science.

Taxation on Hazelton will be his alliance.

Although he'll never spare you two cents,

He is never shy to voice his.

And although Greed is greedy and mentally better,

Deep in his heart, he loves his young brothers.

Born a year later is The Mighty Strength.

All the ladies love this gent.

With golden hair and a chiselled chin,

He surely is one handsome man.

But once the ladies find he's all in his head,

They easily become uninterested.

Strength deeply cares about his people,

But he has one monstrous ego.

He'll carry your bags, and then he'll brag.

He'll lift a wagon, and then he'll brag.

He'll flex his muscles, and then he'll brag.

He'll compare his features, and then he'll…brag!

Yes, we get it, he's physically the best.

But my God, won't he give it a rest?

O, how I hate to introduce this part.

The third brother, and eternal brain fart,

Is Brave. He is one team player.

He hopes to become a dragon slayer.

He'll challenge Strength, but he won't win.

He'll even enter a lion's den.

He's never afraid and won't back down,

But his wit has yet to be found.

Young, dumb and risk craved.

Who needs a brain when you're this brave?

And last, but never the least,

Is the man we all dream to be.

Young and full of energy,

Sweet and known to be meek.

Coming out of his yearly shyness,

You must meet The Beloved Kindness!

He may not be strong or even brave,

But he's always there, all will say.

He vowed to be the town's counsellor,

And to help them get over whatever barrier.

But behind that smile and heart of gold,

Kindness will do whatever he's told.

He's easily tricked by his older brothers,

And it may be because he's simply younger.

He lacks wisdom and sophistication.

His kind heart could eradicate him.

He hates to see Hazelton in distress,

So, he'll help no matter the request.

He himself may be depressed,

But declining the people is not of Kindness.

After many decades, Love and Creed passed,

Leaving the town all aghast.

Without their creators there to guide the mass,

The citizens fear their town would collapse.

In which, it did. The people suffered.

The death of their makers made things rougher.

They lost their food and lost their supplier,

Which forced their children up for hire.

The four brothers were filled with exhaust

From working long hours at a low cost.

Until one day came the pope,

Bringing the town of Hazelton hope.

Act I

Scene I. Hazelton

Narrator:

The citizens of Hazelton scramble around,

Expressing their weary for the town.

'Twas hot yet cold on a fizzy May

As they make it through the busy day.

Kindness kissed his wife in bed,

And then he softly touched her head.

He opened his door without a frown,

And went about helping his town.

Old Woman:

Kindness! Kindness!

Where is Kindness?

Kindness:

I'm here maiden.

And thou request?

Old Woman:

I think my husband is abstinent.

We have barely been intimate.

I've seen signs of impotence.

Please tell me, what do you suggest?

Kindness:

I understand your lack of sleep,

But I am quite busy.

This is beyond my level of expertise.

I think it's best that you consult with Greed.

Narrator:

Kindness quickly walks away from the awkward situation

As a young boy stops him in desperation.

Young Boy:

Sir Kindness, won't thou assist?

Kindness:

Yes, young lad. What is it?

Young Boy:

Well, there's this girl in my class,

And she's a beautiful lass.

Gee, she's a beauty! No doubt!

I want to ask her out,

But…

Kindness:

But what, kiddo?

Young Boy:

I dunno…

I'm not the best-looking person out here.

Kindness:

And that is something she shouldn't care.

Narrator:

Kindness placed his hand on the child's shoulder

And then he softly pulled him closer.

Kindness:

What makes a great partner is never the feature,

But kindness, loyalty, a listener, a teacher.

And if it were looks that ever mattered,

Strength would be on top of the ladder.

What you need is more confidence.

And besides, I think you're a charming gent.

Young Boy:

Thank you, Kindness!

Kindness:

I wish you the best.

Narrator:

The Boy and Kindness hug and depart

After speaking heart to heart.

Ladies of the town gather in amazement

As they watch Strength do his daily assignments.

Lady 1:

Look! There he is!

Lady 2:

O, it's Strength!

Narrator:

Strength smiles and waves. Then a barrel, he lifts

With only one hand. He blows a kiss.

Lady 3:

Wow, he is strong!

Lady 1:

And his arms are so long!

Lady 2:

O Strength, I think I need your help!

I need to be carried; I'm not feeling well.

Young Mother:

Out of the way, ditzy girl!

Strength, my son fell down a well.

Lady 3:

Wait your turn! I was here first!

Lady 1:

No, I was here first!

Lady 2:

But I was here first!

Narrator:

The ladies and mother fight for the position

To be the first to give Strength a mission.

Strength:

Ladies please, one at a time.

Sir Salas:

Strength, I'm in need of your might.

Narrator:

Sir Salas rushes past the whores

As Strength is greatly bombarded with chores.

Strength:

O, Sir Salas! That is, you, wow?

I knew one day you'd come around.

You've something for me, lost to be found?

You've come to congratulate me on our last contest?

Or you've come to say that I am the best.

You've finally realised I am your last resort.

What problem have you of the sort?

Sir Salas:

We all know that my arms were damaged.

That is the only reason why you won the sport.

And even with your firm advantage,

You will never be my last resort.

Young Mother:

Can we please stop this arguing?

My son fell down the well and he's drowning.

Brave:

Don't worry mummy,

I'll save your honey!

Strength:

And there goes the dummy.

Narrator:

Brave dove down after the child with hope,

Then Strength went down to save them both.

They rose from the water gasping for air.

Strength placed them on the ground then brushed his hair.

Lady 1, 2, and 3:

Whoo-hoo!

Bravo, Strength!

Strength:

I thought you knew you cannot swim.

Brave:

I thought you knew to let me win.

Strength:

When it comes to harmful circumstances,

Let me be the one to chance it.

You go see about Kindness; he's been acting strange all morning.

Maybe you can help him with whatever he is mourning.

Narrator:

Brave removed water from his hair and ear,

Then he departed to find Kindness near.

Greed exited his office with papers in hand,

Then he was stopped by an angry man.

Man:

Greed, Greed, Greed! I'm greatly stunned.

I'm seeing a decrease in my funds.

I'm wondering what wrong could be…

Greed:

I do not a service without a fee.

You need me to manage your currency,

You must pay whatever's pending.

Man:

I understand…

Greed:

Then move your hand!

Narrator:

Greed shrugged the man's hand from his shoulder.

And in his sight, when he looked over,

Were two skinny men moving a boulder.

Or trying to move it, that is.

Greed yelled towards them his unwanted tips.

Greed:

Bending your knees would really help!

But also, exercise and drink some milk.

Narrator:

The old woman hurriedly walks up to Greed

With the same problem Kindness could not relieve.

Old Woman:

Greed, I spoke with Kindness, and he pointed me to you.

My husband isn't sexually involved; I don't know what to do.

Greed:

If I had to wake up every morning and turn to you,

Best believe I'd be abstinent, too.

Narrator:

The woman gasped in disbelief

As Greed stomped away cockily.

Brave entered Kindness' post to speak

As his last citizen finally leaves.

Citizen:

Thank you, Kindness.

Kindness:

I wish you the best.

Narrator:

Brave noticed the distraught look on Kindness' face.

He leans in closer and sincerely says:

Brave:

Kindness?

Kindness:

Brave…yes?

Brave:

O, it's just… you seem off today.

Kindness:

No, I'm the same as any other day.

Brave:

Strength sent me here to talk.

Maybe we can go for a walk?

Kindness:

No. My business is none of yours.

And besides, what could I need you for…

…I'm sorry.

Brave:

Don't worry.

It is true after all.

Kindness:

No, Brave. I was wrong.

Brave:

Well, I'm useless to this town.

I couldn't save a kid who was going to drown.

I'm…

I am supposed to be listening to you, not crying about me.

Strength told me there is something you're mourning.

Kindness:

No, I'm fine.

I think he was trying to push you away.

He's been very busy since…the day.

You're a liability to him.

But to me, you're a gem.

Narrator:

The brothers exchanged warming smiles,

Then they heard a loud rumbling from a mile.

They exit the office and see a pile

Of citizens surrounding Greed and Strength.

Very angry are the people of Hazelton,

Chattering, moaning, griping, and complainin'.

Lady 1:

I need help with my wagon!

Strength:

Ladies! Ladies! Calm down!

Young Mother:

My son fell down the well again!

Brave:

Where!? I'll save him! He mustn't drown!

Lady 2:

Where is my money!

Greed:

Hey!

Young Mother:

My son is drowning!

Kindness:

Wait!

Man 1:

Where is Brave?

Brave:

Say!?

Pope:

STOP THIS MADNESS!

Narrator:

The pope yelled in a vexed vibe,

And entered the circle of a complexed tribe.

Pope:

We are not where our founders had us.

Look at this mess!

Running around in distress.

We mustn't let the death of Love and Creed,

Leave us to be in such need.

Citizen:

Well, we need someone to keep us orderly,

And we can't have that without Creed.

We may pray to your heavens above,

But who are we without Love?

All Citizens:

Yeah!

Pope:

You are the people of Hazelton!

You are privileged with four great men,

Yet, you still find a way to be indigent.

But I understand.

The passing of their mother and father has struck us all deeply,

And being frantic makes things seem easy.

So, I've come to you all with glad tidings

With a letter I've found in my papacy.

I shall read to you all the buoyant writings

From our belated Love and Creed.

Narrator:

The citizens begin whispering

As the brothers look around confusingly.

Pope:

"To our beloved children: Greed, Kindness, Brave, and Strength,

By the time you read this sorrowful note, hopefully you've become men.

For only a man can accept our death and move on to be the protector of Hazelton.

We believed the passing of at least one of us

Would cause a bit of a fuss.

We decided a throne shall be contended for,

To be sure Hazelton will be insured.

We simply could not choose which of you to rule,

Knowing one of you would be overruled,

And another would be simply fooled.

And the other would be outrageously rude,

And then the other wouldn't know what to do!

So, we shouldn't leave it up to you.

The people of Hazelton must come together

And vote for whichever brother,

To be the first King of Hazelton.

And may the best man win.

But whoever it shall be,

Will you promise us, please,

To not let the title 'King'

Fill you with conceit?

And always remember

Who you are without your brothers,

And what is a king

To his family.

Protect each other evermore.

We love you four, one never more."

Greed:

Pass me this!

Narrator:

Greed did insist.

He snatched the paper from the pope,

And fixed his well sewn robe.

The brothers began fighting over the note,

As the citizens watched along with hope.

Strength:

No, I shall read it.

Brave:

Let me read it!

Greed:

You couldn't if you tried.

Kindness:

May I?

Narrator:

Kindness walked up to Greed and Greed handed him the will.

Kindness read it thoroughly, standing ever so still.

His older brothers noticed his weary.

His deep brown eyes started to get teary.

Kindness:

I cannot participate in such activities.

I'm-I'm quite busy.

Greed:

Fine! Then it'll be us three.

Brave:

No, no, no. What? What is this?

What's going on, Kindness?

Kindness:

It's just, I have a wife and kids.

And being a king

Would overwhelm me.

Brave:

No, that is not it.

I cannot be tricked.

There's something you're hiding,

And know you can trust me.

Strength:

No matter what it is,

You made a promise.

You must compete, Kindness.

Do you want to let our parents down?

Someone like you deserves the crown.

Our city is in deep trouble,

But you'd turn them away for your own struggles?

That is not of kindness,

That is selfishness.

You must compete.

Narrator:

Kindness thought for a while in defeat.

He looked around at the citizens,

Then over to the pope again.

The pope nodded his head towards him.

Kindness looked back at Strength.

Kindness:

I agree.

Pope:

Voting will take place in three days morning,

After The Few give their opening statements.

They must convince you this next morning

Why they should be king and their parent's replacement.

Narrator:

The pope, the citizens, as well as The Few,

Carried on doing whatever they do.

Although he agreed to,

Kindness didn't want to.

But for his parents he must do.

Scene II. Candidacy Stage

Narrator:

'Tis a sunny day at Hazelton's bay,

And the citizens gathered around the stage.

They watched the brothers enter and wave,

And instructions, the pope began to explain.

Pope:

Come here poor children,

And listen to your men.

Today the brothers must explain

Why they feel they should be King of Hazelton.

The citizens are in charge of this campaign,

As the brothers take turns, one by one.

You may ask questions about their future rulings

Or even questions about their character.

You may question their past doings.

You may question them on whatever.

Introducing the first to compete,

The eldest sons of Love and Creed,

Strength and Greed.

Narrator:

The citizens clapped as Greed stepped up.

His heavy footsteps removed the dust

From the old wooden stage.

He saw people holding scrolls of his name

And Hazelton flags as they cheer and wave.

The brown stage creaks with every step he takes.

The citizens did silence as Greed did pace.

Greed:

I think it is quite obvious that I am your choice.

I am richer, older,

Wiser, and bolder.

My opening statement, I do not need to voice.

You are ill and dying.

My skills are undying.

What the city needs is financial aid,

And I am the only one able to pay.

Strength:

Ladies and gentlemen,

I am Strength.

I am the strongest amongst.

Every day it is me you trust,

With anything you cannot lug.

I've helped the elderly up the hills.

Greed:

But it is me who heals the ill.

He can carry you up the mountain,

But he brings you to me for medicine.

Even he relies on me.

Would you want a king who's always in need?

I am smart, wise, intelligent, and wealthy.

Those are things you must perceive in a king.

And with my funds I can repair our roads.

I can buy us crops and buy us loads,

Loads of loaves and loads of clothes.

Our minors are currently working for pay,

Constructing buildings along our pave'.

I can hire workers from another country

To do our work and to feed the hungry.

Man:

But you've had riches all this time.

Why is it now that you want to chime?

Strength:

Because he doesn't, kind sir.

He won't even lend to his brothers.

And if you choose him to be king,

He will find a way to take your things.

Taxing the poor while loving himself,

A man like him shall burn in hell!

Greed:

If we're talking about loving oneself,

You're listening to a man who does so well.

Narrator:

The citizens laugh at Greed's statement

As Strength looks towards Greed in embarrassment.

Strength looks over at the roaring crowd

And continued his argument without a frown.

Strength:

Ladies and gents, I do lustfully love myself

Deeply. I agree, I need some help.

But rather you a man who's overconfident

Than a man who is covetous?

People of Hazelton,

You need my strength.

For if a deadly beast were released on this village,

Who would you call on, a man of greed or a man of strength?

One of us would take our things and run away,

While the other will fight and is here to stay.

So, my kind people, cast your vote for me

And let me be your very first king.

Narrator:

The citizens clap and cheer for Strength

Ending the first round of their argument.

Pope:

We will take a third ten's break

Before we listen to Kindness and Brave.

Narrator:

The pope and brothers all exit the stage.

Scene III. Forbidden Temple

Narrator:

Strength stomped towards Greed backstage

To hear why he misbehaved.

Greed pulled tobacco from his pant

And lit it with a nearby lamp.

Strength:

What happened there, Greed?

Greed:

What dost thou show?

Strength:

Your behaviour was rudely keen.

Brave:

I agree. I know.

Kindness:

And don't turn your cheek!

Strength:

And what is that smoking?

Narrator:

Greed took a puff from his tobacco

And then he untied his robe.

Greed:

THIS is a cigar, I invented it.

And THAT was a competition.

Brave:

May I try some of it?

Narrator:

Kindness moved Braves hand.

Strength:

Greed, we can compete

Without being mean.

Greed:

I did not make the rules, Strength.

It is the people we must convince.

And if you cannot take a bit of heat,

I suggest you rethink being King.

Narrator:

Greed passed his cigar to Brave

And giddy Brave became.

Greed left with nothing else to say,

And Strength began to become irate.

Kindness:

This is only a competition, Strength.

I'm sure Greed is doing whatever he can to win.

Remember, he's always been competitive.

Strength:

It does not matter who will win.

All I know is I'm better than him…

…And I better win.

Narrator:

Strength, as well, walked away.

Kindness then turned to Brave.

Kindness:

Brave,

Put that away!

Narrator:

Brave tossed the cigar into a vase.

Kindness:

Follow me into the temple.

There may be something in our parents' will.

Something that can help us with this contest.

Because I feel I may not be able to rest.

Narrator:

Kindness and Brave mounted their horses.

They journeyed through Hazelton to search for sources.

They were eager to enter the forbidden land.

There were goosebumps on each of their hands.

They passed by ladies who wished them well.

They passed men with goods to sell.

They passed children running around fountains.

They travelled through and up the mountains.

And from afar, they peeked at the temple.

They entered, though punishment was potential.

The temple had such a beautiful structure:

Curves, points, and vibrant colours.

The pillars were white with golden indents.

The roof was patterned with golden rims.

Green, blue, silver, and orange,

Were splashed around the door and hinge.

The temple ran as wide as the greatest ocean.

It also stood tall like The Mighty Strength.

They adored every single incision.

And in awe, they continued their mission.

Brave and Kindness jumped off their saddles.

They paced across the floral land.

The green grass kissed their toes through their sandals.

The dry warm wind circled around their hands.

Kindness kissed the flowers with his lips.

And the cool water, Brave did sip.

They trotted up the steps and stopped at the door.

Kindness opened it; the white dust fell to the floor.

The decorative interior was chillingly silent,

They heard their footsteps echo.

Every step they took seemed to be violent

As they examined the forbidden temple.

They slowly walked up to a velvet throne,

And with excitement, Brave made it his own.

Brave:

Ahh, Kindness! It's so comfortable.

It's so beautiful.

Kindness:

It's so colourful.

Narrator:

Kindness looked over at a glass case.

And into it, reflected his face.

He saw a golden crown embedded with gems.

The sun beamed off the crown and onto him.

The beauty of the crown nearly blinded Kindness.

He reached towards it and removed the glass case.

He slowly lifted up the crown and placed it upon his head.

The crown slid down and covered his face.

Kindness:

It is quite large for me.

But you, let us see.

Narrator:

After letting him admire the jewelled headdress,

Brave stood tall to be dressed by Kindness.

Kindness placed the crown onto Brave

As they both looked into a mirror with crave.

Kindness:

Ah, look at you Brave. You look just like dad.

Eyes of emerald, hair of sand.

And you in this crown, I think I'm in love.

Brave:

It fits like a glove.

Kindness:

Yes, it does…

…Suspiciously.

Brave:

Deliciously!!

Kindness:

Ironically…

Brave:

Superstonically!

Kindness:

That is not a word.

Brave:

You're not a word!

Narrator:

Kindness had his suspicions.

But the crown didn't matter, he was on a mission.

Kindness:

Come quick, Brave, and put that back.

We must stay on track.

Narrator:

Kindness led Brave into the Hall

Where a desk with papers is what he saw.

He glanced over at a stone model

Where he noticed something quite awful.

Kindness:

The robe on this mannequin is missing!

Brave:

You mean the one weareth Greed?

Kindness:

…That's exactly what I mean.

Narrator:

Kindness examined the Hall looking for clues

While Brave admired every view.

The gold paint traced the windows.

Feathers stuffed in linen pillows.

The smell of pine was faintly present.

The flying dust was vaguely pigmented.

The marbled floor was waxed in iridescent.

The stone walls were deeply indented.

Kindness walked up to a desk and opened the drawer,

And inside it, a chest and more.

He picked up the brown box and opened it carefully.

He found a torn letter and read it thoroughly.

Kindness' eyes embiggened but then he frowned.

He couldn't believe what he had found.

And without a word, he folded the paper.

He placed it in his pouch and his eyes tapered.

He picked up the box to put it back in the drawer,

But then he noticed the lock and scores.

He saw missing screws and a random scratch

As if someone had busted through the latch.

In this temple, someone had entered.

And the beloved riches have been tampered.

Kindness:

Brave we must go, I'm sure they are all worried.

We've been gone for a while. We must scurry.

Brave:

But what does that note in your bag?

Kindness:

O, it's just a reminder of dad.

Narrator:

The two young brothers rode back to the stage.

But there was a secret Kindness never gave.

Scene IV. Candidacy Stage

Narrator:

Kindness and Brave make it back to the stage.

Strength:

You're awfully late, Kindness and Brave.

Kindness:

We were just looking through…

Brave:

The forbidden temp…

Kindness:

Template!

Ugh, yes. The forbidden templates.

They belong to Greed, and they're forbidden.

We found those we needed.

Strength:

Hmmm…It's your turn on the stage.

Narrator:

Strength walked away.

Brave:

Why did you lie?

Kindness:

Because it is forbidden!

We're lucky to be alive.

Let's hope to be forgiven.

Narrator:

All of the brothers crossed the stage

As the Pope introduced Kindness and Brave.

Brave stepped up, grinning ear to ear.

The citizens stopped chatting for a clearer hear.

The silence made Brave greatly nervous.

He swallowed saliva and sweated his surface.

He pulled his pants up over his large gut.

He closed his eyes and inhaled the dust.

Then, from the crowd and very loud,

A woman questioned to help him out.

Woman 1:

What qualities do you hold to be a king?

Brave:

Well, I'm brave.

Narrator:

Brave smiled brightly.

Greed and Strength stood back and laughed.

Kindness noticed the empathy they lacked.

The people of Hazelton looked at each other.

They continued to question the dumb brother.

Woman 2:

What hath you to provide?

Man 1:

What art thou talents?

Woman 3:

Why shall we confide?

Man 2:

Can you bring us balance?

Narrator:

The yearning citizens were drilling into Brave

Like a woodpecker would to a sweet gum tree.

He stuttered much but had nothing to say.

Then Kindness stepped up and began to speak.

Kindness:

My brother here has no talent.

He's not strong, rich, kind, nor vibrant.

But every morning he wakes up with positivity,

And thinks of ways to help his city.

He doesn't complain, he doesn't back down.

And someone so brave deserves a crown.

Man 3:

Are you surrendering your chance of being royal?

Kindness:

No, I'm giving you insight on who is loyal.

Brave and I, we're very much alike.

We don't focus on ourselves; we don't care about our money.

The people in this audience make us feel…

Brave:

Sunny!

Kindness:

We wake up with a purpose and put our differences aside.

We toss away our problems and keep you all in mind.

So, what makes a king is neither his smartness, richness, nor neither his strength,

But compassion, commitment, and the heart he holds within.

Ladies and gentlemen, you have four options but do caution.

I advise you not to choose the man who will treat you as an option.

I advise you not to choose the man who will sell you in an auction.

Narrator:

The crowd mumbled and pondered the event.

The sun went down, and they were dismissed.

Pope:

If you have no further questions,

You all may go home and prepare for judgments.

In tomorrow's a.m., we must return

And the citizens must express their concerns.

Narrator:

The pope concluded and closed the city.

Strength walked up to his younger siblings.

Strength:

That's quite the connection you two have there.

You two skedaddle off for quite some time and make it back here,

Holding hands, supporting each other.

Why do you stick together?

Kindness:

Because we're brothers.

Brave:

And that's what brothers do.

Kindness:

Yes, Brave, so true.

Narrator:

Kindness walked off with Brave as Strength stared at them with jealousy.

Then from behind him walked up Greed.

Strength:

Those two are so far up each other's posterior.

Greed:

And why dost thou care? Art thou superior?

Narrator:

The brothers departed in the evening.

Strength felt somewhat lonely.

He had no connections with any of his siblings,

He realised they each had a falling.

Scene **V**. Lake of Love

Narrator:

The night sky was deep blue with stars scattered about,

And it's holding a crescent moon and just a few white clouds.

The moon reflected across the beautiful lake, the one created by Love.

Brave and Strength walked under the sky and cherished the sights above.

Strength:

It's a beauty, this lake.

You know, we've always been told about the memories it makes.

As if this lake holds some sort of power to bring relief.

It brings one joy and love. It makes one happy.

Brave:

Is that why you bring me?

Narrator:

Strength looked over and saw two long sticks.

He picked them up and tossed one to Brave.

Strength:

Say, remember this?

Remember the games we'd play?

Narrator:

Strength squatted down in a fighting stance.

Brave swung his stick, and of course, missed.

With smiles on their faces, they fought and danced.

For the first time in years, they felt like kids.

Strength:

Take that, you foul beast!

Brave:

Take this, you hideous cheat!

Narrator:

Strength swept Brave's legs and flattened him.

He placed his sixteen-inch foot on Brave's chest.

He raised his stick sword and hollered a hymn.

He declared himself to be named the best.

Brave:

Okay Strength, you won.

Strength:

Of course, I did, I always do.

I am the chosen one!

Narrator:

Strength helped Brave up from the grass of dew.

Brave:

Um…Strength?

Strength:

Yes?

Narrator:

Strength was busy gazing at his reflection in the lake.

For him to be fond of his outer beauty, not long did it take.

Brave:

I've never thought you'd be so kind to me.

It seemed that you were only interested in being king.

Strength:

Well of course, I am. I'm going to win. I'm better than all. I-

But I think you are very well.

You're doing a great job, Brave, at whatever it is you…dwell.

Look…don't be hard on yourself.

I know I may come off as uneasy to deal with,

But you have just as great as an advantage.

Brave:

No one believes in me.

You saw how they questioned me.

I have nothing.

Strength:

That's not true. You have bravery.

You have us three. You have this city.

Even I get scared to do some things,

That's why I push the duty on you.

I could never do the things you do.

I believe in you.

Brave:

I love you.

Strength:

You're only saying that because this is the Lake of Love. Mother bestowed some sort of witchery to make us have deep feelings.

Brave:

It makes us feel what we were already feeling but hiding.

They are not forced, these feelings.

Strength:

Those might have been the smartest words I've ever heard from you.

Brave:

I love you.

Scene VI. Judgement Day Stage

Narrator:

As the brothers wait for the Pope's introduction,

They ponder backstage and carry discussions.

Kindness noticed Brave's absence,

But before he could speak, Greed insisted on his assistance.

Greed:

You there! Artless and wretched dope.

I need your help with adjusting my robe.

What is a king with a poor wardrobe?

I mustn't step out looking as so.

Narrator:

Kindness walked up to assist his elder.

He placed the robe over Greed's shoulders.

Kindness:

Absolutely, Greed.

I believe you could have asked me nicely.

Greed:

Tuh! Niceness is the reason why you are so stressed.

Having thick skin is what I know best.

Show no mercy, show no care.

Then you'll see who really cares.

Those who stick around even when you're mean

Are the only ones worth to keep.

Why dost thou think I've lesser problems?

Ask me for help? They don't even bother.

Ask you for help? They see no problem.

We know which one of us will make it farther.

Keep the less close to you.

It will make you look great, 's'what I do.

Narrator:

Kindness ignored Greed's terrible advice

And decided to address the obvious sights.

Kindness:

Where is Brave?

Narrator:

Kindness asked while knotting the cape.

Greed:

Retrieving a pendant

From a serpent…

…For a citizen.

Narrator:

Greed turned to the mirror to admire himself.

He caught Kindness' reflection as well.

Greed:

You're ruining my visuals.

Kindness:

As usual.

Narrator:

As Kindness turned to walk away,

With a swollen face, entered Brave.

Brave:

Greed, I finally defeated the snake.

Greed:

Ah, thanks.

Narrator:

Greed palmed his pendant and pocketed it.

Leaving Kindness to deal with Brave's wounds.

Kindness:

Not one medicine did he offer us.

Here, let me see what I can do.

Brave:

Thank you Kindness, I'm excited for today.

I can't wait to hear what they'll say!

Kindness:

Well, it is Judgement Day.

I think I'm a bit afraid.

Narrator:

The brothers and pope entered the stage

And the citizens gathered around.

The pope held up his crooked cane

And weakly stomped it down.

The shark of citizens suddenly silenced

And the pope started his sentence.

Pope:

Today is the second day,

It brings us Judgement Day.

After hearing their statements yesterday,

You all must give your say.

Judge them for their future and present,

But keep in mind their past.

Let us keep this event pleasant

And be thoughtful for what is asked.

Who will be the first to judge these fine men?

Please, raise your hand.

Narrator:

The citizens jump up and down,

Screaming at the pope to be chosen.

The pope pointed towards a woman found

Swarming through the dozens.

Pope:

What is your name, lady?

Sella:

I am Sella B.

I would like to thank Strength and Brave,

For their nephew has been saved.

He was drowning in a nearby well when they came to save his life.

His father was nowhere to be found, nowhere in sight.

Strength:

Did you say that child is our nephew?

Sella:

Yes, I did. It is true.

Brave:

He doesn't look like Kindness' son, Pete.

Sella:

Because he isn't, he's Greed's.

Narrator:

The citizens and brothers gasped and mumble

As Greed rolled his eyes and began to stumble.

Greed:

You are a very, very, VERY unfair woman.

I would never lie down with such a hag!

And if I did, I'd remember the moment.

The thought of placing my eyes upon you makes me gag!

Narrator:

The crowd griped towards Greed's attitude.

Man 1:

Say, that was rude.

Lady 1:

He wasn't with you because he was fondling me!

Narrator:

The crowd silenced once more.

Lady 1:

He whispered things, things so sweet.

He got what he wanted and he hit the door!

Lady 2:

He impregnated me with twins,

And before I knew it, he was gone with the wind!

Lady 3:

Junior grew up without his father,

And to vote him as king, I would not bother.

He can't even take care of his own children!

What makes you think he'll take care of Hazelton?

Brave:

Yes, we see.

He is not fit to be King.

Greed:

Silence yourself, you pitiful being!

Ladies, ladies, can we please,

Put our differences aside for this eve?

Sella B:

Differences!?

These are your children!

Greed:

There's no verification that he is mine!

Lady 1:

Look at his eyes!

You need to take us more seriously!

Strength:

Yes, Greed, I agree.

Your help is what these ladies need.

Greed:

Look, just because these tramps move around

And the father of their kids cannot be found,

Does not mean I am responsible for them.

And besides, a few of them were just stands.

How could one time get them expectant?

Kindness:

I think you should help them at least.

I mean, you are running to be king.

Brave:

Yeah, a king never lets his people down.

These girls need you more than you a crown.

Greed only cares about his money.

He'll never share with his city.

Strength:

Brave, let's take it easy.

Maybe Greed can change, go on let's see.

Narrator:

Greed looked at his brothers then out to the crowd.

The ladies of anger were all around.

This was his chance to fix his truancy.

He wanted nothing more than to be King.

He stepped up to the edge of the stage.

Greed:

Ladies and people of every age.

I have given you many things:

Maths, medicine, science, expertise.

What more can this city need?

Look to your right at these three,

Very talented, but it is me.

Me whom you all need.

'Tis why you're begging me.

I'll help you find the fathers of your infants.

But I assure you, I am not him.

Brave:

He's given you all those things.

But he's yet to give you money.

Narrator:

Greed scowled towards Brave.

His face was red, and his teeth were clenched.

His eyebrows were caved,

And curled were his lips.

Greed:

I'll give them something.

Lady 4:

He's offered me and his kids nothing!

No clothes, no food, no currency!

You've been having fun and being wild.

I need some support to take care of our child.

Greed:

If it is my money thou want, you'll never get it!

Brave:

He just admitted it!

Greed:

No! 'Tis not what I meant!

Strength:

Well, what did you mean?

Brave:

That he's old, withered, and a deadbeat.

Greed:

BRAVE!!

Brave:

Greed?

Greed:

Let us proceed with someone else.

Someone who cannot justify himself.

Man 2:

Oh yes, Brave.

What a strange name.

A man who is never afraid,

But when the time comes for questioning, he's nothing to say.

Brave:

Well, I've a lot to say actually.

Like, how I'm feeling shappy.

Kindness:

Brave, you're not helping.

Greed:

Oh no, do not help him, Kindness.

I mean look at him, Brave is a mess.

Hazelton needs more than bravery.

Kindness:

But what they don't need is you, Greed.

Man 1:

Say?

But do we need someone who we can easily persuade?

You never wanted to compete, but you couldn't stand your ground.

Why would we vote you as king when you don't even want the crown?

Kindness:

It's not that I do not want it,

But I cannot have it.

I have things you all do not wish.

Is it not enough for me to disregard my family to be here in this competition?

Is it not enough for me to care for you first than to care for my wife and kids?

I'm more than just your counsellor, I am a husband and a dad.

There are things that you have that I wish I had:

Freedom, sleep, happiness in a heap.

Greed leaves home to be king for himself, I leave home to be king for justice.

He has families he cares nothing for, I have a family I'm begging to be with.

But even if…

Even if my family needs me more, Hazelton is at the top of my list.

And you will always be.

Narrator:

After sharing his heartfelt message, the citizens sobbed in quiet.

Strength:

Absolute beauty.

I guess I should quit.

There he goes playing his cards of 'which brother cares most'.

You need more than care, money, and hope.

I have just as much money and twice the bravery.

I have all the cares, but they don't have strength.

There's no need to look further than me,

I am where it is.

Lady 2:

O please, what do you know about care?

Sir Salas:

You go on bragging about how you have good hair.

You believe that you're the best here.

Strength:

Because I am!

You've tried lifting three barrels with one hand like me and you broke a limb!

There are things you can't do and that is why I do them.

Everything my brothers are, I am all in one plus more!

I am everything you all have ever looked for!

Lady 3:

We cannot stand your constant gloat.

What you brag about, we already know.

Greed has more money than us both,

But he does not make us feel broke.

Sir Salas:

A man with a dangerous ego

Is not meant to rule a mass of people!

Strength:

Veto! Veto! Veto! Veto!

Veto me and what I am to be.

Not meant to rule thus say unto me.

Questioning, questioning, questioning.

Thou art questioning Love and Creed,

The creators of thee, the creators of me.

For you to say what you believe,

You purport the purpose of who I am.

Not in royalty, I rule the land.

As one fourth of the protectors,

I am definite.

And you Salas, you sir,

Have broken a commandment:

"Never deny a 'Promising Few',

Never deny the things he do.

Never take away from who he is.

Never declare what he is not meant."

Therefore I, a 'Promising Few', declare the Bobbies and Peelers

To take Sir Salas to the Dungeon of Dealers…

And let it be said he was placed and convicted by Strength.

Narrator:

The Bobbies came and stormed the event.

The citizens gasped in fear as they took Salas.

They locked him away, but Greed was impressed.

Greed:

Now, that was powerful.

Dangerously powerful.

Lady Salas:

That was my husband! We have children!

Strength:

He should've respected me and Hazelton.

Kindness:

Strength, how could you? He has a family.

For him to be taken, there was no need.

Strength:

He broke a commandment made to protect us! Don't tell me you're questioning our parents as well.

Kindness:

He spoke his opinion, and I believe in free will!

Those commandments weren't placed to protect you or me,

They were placed to control this city!

Strength:

So, what dost thou say? Abolish The Commandments?

Kindness:

If I were king, that's what I would suggest!

Strength, these people are not puppets.

Strength:

But thou art.

You would do anything they beg of you even if it tears you apart.

A king is not supposed to do what's right, but what's best.

And it seems you're too sincere to understand, Kindness.

It's quite ill to have you as a part of this contest,

Like an unwanted tumour in a lady's breast.

You know, I fear you love being controlled,

Love always doing what's told.

And that is why I will always feel sorry for the woman who calls you "lover".

Because you love these pitiful people, more than you love her.

Where is she anyway? I can't seem to find her out.

She may be dumb enough to stay with you, but we three can do without.

Narrator:

The citizens mourned in disappointment.

They could not believe The Mighty Strength.

Kindness:

If that is true, Strength, that you can do without me,

Remember these words when you lose your strength.

Remember this battle when I become king,

And remember this moment when I am deceased.

Narrator:

Kindness, with rare anger, exited the stage

Leaving Strength with unforgettable remorse.

Strength felt sorry and it showed on his face,

But he will never admit it, of course.

Lady 2:

Strength, you have made some very good points.

But at the end of the day, you always disappoint.

Narrator:

Strength looked towards the crowd of disgusted citizens.

He examined them with deep confusion.

Strength:

Is this not a competition?

Is this not what you're here for?

Greed made a fool of me a day ago, and you all found it humorous.

But how dare I stand on this same stage and tell Kindness he's tumorous?

How dare I stand here and point out the blatant truth?

Lady Salas:

And send someone to the dungeon, how dare you?

Lady 1:

This is Judgement Day, where we speak freely.

Had we known The Commandments were not exempt, we wouldn't've agreed.

Narrator:

Greed leaned over and whispered to Strength.

Greed:

The people are on the same wavelength.

Thou art in trouble from what I can tell.

Before they elect, atone with Kindness,

But do it for yourself.

Pope:

I believe that is enough judgement for the day.

Let us give the brothers some time to fix their mistakes.

They have some rekindling to do, and you have votes to make.

Your votes will be counted and read by me the next day.

Narrator:

The brothers and citizens finish their meeting.

Strength goes out to search for Kindness.

Greed:

Brave! I have another quest for thee.

Brave:

O gee! I wonder what is next!

Narrator:

Strength walked all through Hazelton.

He noticed the evil glares from citizens.

He paid it no mind since he believed

He was doing whatever it took to be king.

He approached Kindness' little house.

He knocked on the door and waited a while.

The door opened and in a white blouse,

Was a little girl with the brightest smile.

Priscilla:

Uncle Strength! What brings you here?

Strength:

I'm here to speak to your father, dear.

Priscilla:

Pete! Come quick!

Look at this!

Pete:

Whoa! Uncle Strength.

Narrator:

Pete ran to the door and looked up to the sky.

He and Priscilla were extremely surprised.

From their perspective, Strength was enormous.

The kids believed he was a giant.

His golden hair seemed luminous.

And, to the kids, his eyes were diamonds.

They stood there admiring their handsome relative,

Before Kindness came and interrupted.

Kindness:

Kids, please, go see your mother.

…There's no need for you to be here, brother.

Strength:

I just came here to make amends.

Kindness:

No thank you and stay away from my kids.

Strength:

Kindness, I just…

Narrator:

And the door slammed.

Strength, nervously, wiped his chest.

And before he left, the door opened again.

Kindness:

I forgive you.

Narrator:

Kindness said.

Kindness' kids watched from the back room,

As the brothers stood there in silence.

Strength:

Most of those words, I never meant.

Kindness:

I said, I forgive you.

Scene VII. Voting Stage

Narrator:

A podium was placed with a beautiful crown,

The same crown that Kindness and Brave found,

On the stage on voting day.

The citizens and brothers eagerly wait

For the pope to announce their very first king.

Brave, Strength, Kindness, and Greed,

All stood tall on the stage that day.

Then the pope walked up and began to say:

Pope:

Hear ye! Hear ye! Hear ye! Hear ye!

Late last evening, you all voted.

You thought long and hard about who is truly devoted.

You questioned and listened, and you answered and noted.

And finally, it brings you and me

To the knowing of who our rightful king shall be.

I miscounted the votes the first few times,

But I counted them over, all through the night.

I counted the votes again and again.

I read them over this early mornin'.

I doubled checked them over and then,

After hours and hours of addin' and addin'.

I concluded.

The people have spoken,

And the people have chosen,

For their King of Hazelton to be,

A man so lovely, a man so heavenly.

With beautiful hair

And the fiercest glare,

With an enormous heart, and eyes of glory.

With a grin so mischievous, but a smile so warming.

A man so strong,

A man who's never wrong.

A man never afraid,

A man heaven made.

A man here for us, and we, he saves.

A man here and born to reign.

This man here that you have chosen,

Rich and never outspoken.

And that when we see him, we see green.

He's a man that we all want to be.

A man so wise, a man so manly.

A man so prized, a man so dandy.

Tall and mighty, the prettiest gent.

The man that you all have chosen!

Ladies and gentlemen,

Meet your King of Hazelton!

Young and full of energy,

Sweet and known to be meek.

Finally out of his yearly shyness,

Your very first King of Hazelton, The Beloved Kindness!

Narrator:

The citizens of Hazelton jumped with cheer.

They cheered and shouted, and were glad to hear,

That Kindness was their first king.

But Kindness, well, he seemed,

Disappointed and nervous.

He questioned his purpose.

The pope walked up with the jewelled crown

And placed it upon Kindness' crown.

And just like before, the crown slid down.

He took it off and slightly frowned.

Kindness:

I'm sorry, I cannot take on such responsibilities.

I am not fit for such royal duties.

Narrator:

The audience began whispering and moaning in disgrace.

For Kindness had declined them in their face.

Man 1:

We knew he'd do this! It's such a shame.

Woman 1:

Kindness, he doesn't wear his name!

Strength:

Tuh! Of course not! I deserve to be king!

I am the best, I am great! I am what you need!

I am strong, I am reliable! I am the almighty!

Greed:

Well, if he doesn't want it, give it to me!

Strength:

No! It should go to whoever has the next highest vote.

Pope!?

Pope:

You don't want to know.

Greed:

Ugh! This is unforgivably insane!

Lord, forgive me, for I am about to use your name in vain.

Brave:

Say, Kindness, I'll take the crown!

Greed:

No, thou will not, you inattentive clown!

Strength:

If anyone's inattentive, it's Kindness.

He doesn't care for us.

Kindness:

O, I care for these people as much as you care about yourself.

I'd call you many names, but I fear GOD and hell.

Man 2:

So, who shall be our king? Shall we re-vote?

Greed:

Absolutely, positively, NO!

Woman 1:

So, what exactly are we going to do?

Willa:

I can help you.

Narrator:

Everyone turned to see a view

Of a beautiful woman in the centre of the crowd.

She wore a red robe with a beautiful smile.

Her eyes were brown, and her hair was wild.

Greed:

Who art thou, and speaking without permit?

Willa:

My name is Willa, I'm…a witch.

Narrator:

The citizens screamed, and they backed away.

The witch smiled and began to say:

Willa:

My sister, Nevar, is also a witch.

We both work with black magic.

Nevar is more powerful than I.

I work in public; she works in disguise.

I couldn't help but overhear that you need a solution,

Help with choosing a king for Hazelton.

Pope:

The Few and I are no fools!

We know of the work you two do.

Willa:

Then you should know we've helped you.

We've helped Love and Creed with bearing children.

We've bestowed wonders across the lands.

We've built lands for you all to call home, the home you call '*Hazelton*'.

Greed:

Nevar and Willa, the Witches of Sucrex,

Holding powers from beyond their hex.

I remember the stories our parents used to tell,

But I've always fancied them to be tales.

Willa:

A myth only holds ten percent of the imagination, Greed.

The rest, vrai.

Strength:

O please, stop procrastinating.

What brings you today?

Willa:

Nevar can help you with your decision.

Here is a map to your destination.

Narrator:

The witch threw up her thin scrawny hands,

Red smoke and glitter exploded in the air.

A scroll appeared and flew to where Greed stands.

The citizens moaned, for they were scared.

Greed palmed the scroll and held it firmly.

He looked up at the witch and stood sternly.

Willa:

But before you go on this long-some trip,

I must warn you, be well equipped.

Greed:

Why should we trust in thee?

Willa:

Thus did, Love and Creed.

Narrator:

The witch began to pace around the frightened citizens.

Her red robe dragged across the dusty ground.

She strode up on the stage and walked past Strength.

She paused in front of Greed and examined his frown.

She looked deep into his black eyes and touched his curled moustache.

She admired his pale skin. His short black hair, she massaged.

Willa:

You'll reach my sister's cave,

The Sucrex Cave,

In three weeks time.

The option is presented,

And if you resent it,

That is fine.

Narrator:

The witch spun, and the red smoke returned.

She disappeared as the citizens mourned.

Pope:

Silence, children! Silence.

Brothers, you will not need my guidance.

If you decide to take this route,

I will try my best to help you through.

But those witches have falsified stories.

They destroyed families and murdered cities.

Kindness:

Three weeks time.

That's too long to show.

I need to be with my wife.

I cannot go.

Strength:

This is what our parents want!

They want one of us to be king.

You tell us it's what you do not want,

That you do not want to compete.

Kindness, we are equals, all of us.

You have no choice but to go, it is a must.

Brave:

I think it will be fun! Yes, marvellous!

Strength:

Well, that makes two of us.

Narrator:

Greed stood ever so still, and absolutely quiet.

Questioning his own will, he kept his secret private.

He palmed the scroll tightly, then slowly opened it.

His eyes shrunk and grew as he examined the map.

And just as he thought, it was all a trick.

Their journey to the witch's cave was one awful lap.

But for some odd reason, he doubted his half.

He played it off with a tittered laugh.

Greed:

Well, this journey is long and dangerous,

But it is what our parents ask of us.

They need one of us to be King of Hazelton.

So, I say I am in.

Narrator:

And there was Kindness, left to agree.

Thinking of how long he will grieve.

To go three weeks away from his kids and wife,

That was something he could never try.

He wanted to stand his ground, he wanted to deny the request.

But that was simply not of Kindness.

Kindness:

I guess…

I guess it's for the best.

Narrator:

The brothers and citizens depart from the stage

To prepare themselves for this mysterious journey.

Excited and eager were Strength and Brave,

And, for the crown, Greed was yearning.

But Kindness still could not accept,

The fact that he must participate.

In his heart, he silently wept.

And the trip, he'd not anticipate.

Within hours later, the pope returned with a blacksmith and a few citizens.

Everyone gathered to say goodbye and wish good luck for the beloved gentlemen.

Pope:

As the witch said, you must be well equipped.

And here, unto you, are your noble gifts.

Our bakers and makers have made you dozens

Of bread, fish, nuts, and muffins.

Water and beer that could last you a year,

Clothes and coats for if you get cold.

Wine and swine for your happy nights,

A tent and sheets for if you dare sleep.

Handcrafted by our craftsman,

Boots for your every steppin'.

Handcrafted by our blacksmith,

The finest of all weapons.

These weapons were designed by your parents,

Waiting for you at the perfect moment.

For The Handsome Greed,

From your father, Creed,

A sword and shield

That you shall wield.

Black like your hair and eyes,

Outlined in silver that Creed had mined.

A sheath of leather

That was sewn together

By your very own respected mother.

For The Mighty Strength…

…Nothin'.

You were born with the strongest gift.

With one hand, a house you can lift.

And with muscles stacked along your limbs.

Raise up to the sky, your own two fists,

And show them why you are named Strength.

Now Brave, you're known for your stirring swagger.

Here, I present unto you, two golden daggers.

These daggers are bejewelled with the very gems your mother wore.

She wore them on the day that you were born.

She told us of each stone and their sense,

Hoping you'd understand what they meant.

The pearls as round and white as thee,

Rare and always glistening.

Hold it up to the moon,

And it will tell you what to do.

Hold it up to the sun,

It will tell you what will come.

The rubies, strange but quite unique,

The blood you may shed will always be meek.

Hold it close to your heart,

And you will know when it's time to part.

The sapphire as bright and blue as the sea,

Shall wash away your indignity.

Place it under the freshest of water,

And you will feel the loathe no longer.

There are three stones and two of each,

Use these daggers as often as you need.

And finally, The Beloved Kindness.

I remember when this was addressed.

When your parents saw how precise you could throw,

They presented our craftsman with an arrow and bow.

Your mother weaved this bow in a lovely crescent.

The arch and curves match your smile.

She believed it would be a wonderful present,

And she added these flowers for a simple style.

This string took them years to prepare,

Do you notice it's of your mother's hair?

And your father, he constructed the arrows.

One hundred of these, slick and narrow.

Look at the points, pure silver.

Made from your father's armour.

Take these tools and use them with gratitude.

Use them and go with heroic attitudes!

Farewell brothers and please be safe.

And please beware of the witch's take.

Nevar speaks in riddles, so listen to her carefully.

Think twice before you dare to agree.

Strength:

D'ya hear that? I need not a gift.

I AM STRENGTH!

Narrator:

Strength bragged to his siblings

While, their gifts, they were admiring.

The citizens cheered as the brothers ascended

Their horses, and wished them luck on their mission.

A black horse for Greed, and brown for Strength.

A white horse for Kindness, and for Brave, tan.

They packed their food and weapons presented,

They waved goodbye to the people of Hazelton.

The brothers travelled along a purple pave',

They admired the nature that earth gave.

Red birds and jays flew around their heads.

Butterflies fluttered in yellow and red.

The water sang from the Lake of Love,

The wind hummed from the sky above.

The horses' hooves silently clopped,

Then suddenly, everyone's mood dropped.

They stopped at the entrance of an estranged forest.

They heard a low neigh from a frightened horse.

They saw moss grown over rocks and trees,

And down their spines, they felt a breeze.

The forest was glowing with a dark blue light.

They could've sworn that shadows were in their sight.

Greed pulled out the scrolled map

And he confirmed their first lap.

Greed:

The Fruitful Forest, 'tis where we begin.

Brave:

I can't wait to go in!

Kindness:

I don't think we're prepared for this.

It doesn't seem pleasant.

Brave:

We should go in!

It's the Fruitful Forest, it can't be that bad.

Anything with fruit in it can't be bad.

Strength:

It looks sad.

Kindness:

We should go back.

Brave:

Let's enter the forest!

Strength:

Hold your horses!

Brave:

Our horses are held.

Strength:

Listen to what I am trying to tell.

Kindness:

We should think about this.

Brave:

We should make it quick!

Strength:

You're being overzealous!

Brave:

And you're being overjealous!

Kindness:

That doesn't make sense.

Brave:

You doesn't make sense!

Greed:

And arguing here is no success!

Strength:

Whoa-ho! It's Mr. Smarty-Pants!

A big brain, but bigger bollocks!

Just because you're rich and high in sex,

You think that makes you better than us?

Greed:

Yes! In fact, I'm THE best!

Born sharp-witted, written for success!

And you dare mention my activeness!?

Does my abundance of broads make you jealous?

Hmmm? Zip your lips! Let your tongue be held!

Or I'll take my sword and force a geld!

Brave:

Our horses are girls.

Greed:

Not the horses, you idiot!

Ugh! Let's just move…quick!

Act II

Scene I. The Fruitful Forest

Narrator:

Greed led his younger brothers slowly.

Their horses neighed sadly and lowly.

The leaves on the trees bowed to them as if they were royalty.

The moss on the rocks grew around them as they walked.

Although the leaves seemed to be respectful,

They were dark, torn, and awfully dreadful.

The rocks skipped around with every step their horses took.

They heard whispers in the water from a nearby brook.

Strength:

What's so fruitful about this forest, huh?

It's dark and I've yet to see a berry or plum.

Greed:

Perhaps 'fruitful' has a different understanding:

Not of the fruit, but of the being.

Or maybe this place used to be living,

And mankind destroyed its own meaning.

Narrator:

Suddenly, Kindness fell off his horse and muddy became his clothes.

Brave:

Kindness! What happened? Are you alright?

Kindness:

Yes. I mean no. I think I've been pushed by a ghost.

Greed:

There's no such thing. Control your fright.

Kindness:

I swear it! Something touched my shoulder.

And I heard whispers coming from over-

Narrator:

The brothers heard a tree limb snap.

They jumped from their horses and stood back-to-back.

The brothers formed the most powerful faction.

Brave held up his daggers, ready for action!

Greed hid behind his shield and drew his sword.

Strength rolled up his sleeves without saying a word.

Kindness stood up and aimed an arrow.

Greed squinted his eyes and saw a shadow.

Greed:

Look here! I see it there…

It's…it's a… a…BEARRRR!

Narrator:

Greed jumped in fear and hid behind Strength.

The grizzly roared in horrific suspense.

This big brown bear had sharp yellow teeth.

His dark black eyes matched Greed's.

The bear marched angrily towards his lunch.

Strength wound up his arm for a mighty punch.

Brave jumped in front of Strength with daggers in hand.

Brave:

Step back, Strength!

I've got this!

Narrator:

The bear growled and Brave did, too.

Kindness stepped up to separate the two.

Kindness:

No! Brave!

Wait! Wait! Wait!

Greed:

What dost thou mean, 'wait'? Let him kill the thing!

Kindness:

I believe this creature may be hungry.

Narrator:

Kindness put his hand out and the bear stopped.

It growled some more as Greed sobbed.

It sniffed Kindness' hand and licked his palm.

Kindness:

There, there, creature. Stay calm.

It's okay, we're not here to hurt…thee.

Greed, pass me some fish, slowly.

Greed:

This is our feed!

Kindness:

Then it is us he'll eat!

Narrator:

Greed walked towards his horse and grabbed his sack.

He tossed it towards Kindness, and it landed on the ground.

The bear crouched over and sniffed the snack.

It began munching on fish, loudly in sound.

The brothers silently ascended their horses,

Then, they carefully exited the forest.

Greed:

I'm a bit bummed, that bear was a bore.

I wanted to use my beautiful sword.

Strength:

You shouldn't have given him all of our fish.

Just a couple should've been his dish.

Greed:

It doesn't matter. We're all safe, you see?

And it's all thanks to me!

Kindness:

Of course, Greed.

Scene II. City of Hahm

Narrator:

The Few travelled far along the purple road,

But Greed had trouble finding where to go.

Greed:

I fear, young brothers, we may be lost.

City of Hahm is where we must cross.

Brave:

Hey, I thought you were smart.

Greed:

Brave! Please, do not start.

Kindness:

May I take a look at the map, Greed?

Greed:

Sure, but it won't do any deed.

Narrator:

Kindness examined the map, close and carefully.

He tilted and turned it, and held it fiddly.

He squinted his eyes and scratched his chin.

He put down the map and saw a maiden.

Kindness:

Ah, look! A citizen.

Maybe she can tell us where to begin.

Narrator:

Kindness handed Greed the map.

They led their horses along the path.

As they were getting close to the lone female.

They noticed that she was not well.

From five feet away, they saw her face.

She was so unkept, it should be a disgrace.

She was dirty and raggedy,

Something they had never seen.

They could see her hands slowly turning green.

And when they approached her, she had a terrible stench.

A stench so foul, they couldn't bear.

Spoiled rotten was this ugly wench.

To ask for directions, they wouldn't dare.

Strength:

I think she's dead.

Greed:

She should be dead.

A woman like that should never be wed.

Kindness:

Hello, madam!

Narrator:

Kindness said.

He jumped off his horse and looked down at the hag.

She sat on the ground protecting her bag.

Brave:

Say, you shouldn't be out here alone off the grid.

Kindness:

Excuse my brother, his brain is obtunded.

Madam?

We are looking for directions to The City of Hahm.

Do you think you could point us in the right direction?

We are on an important mission.

Hag:

Yes, yes, I can. I will.

But, can you please give me a meal?

Greed:

Nope! Not today!

Kindness:

Of course, we can. We have some to spare.

Narrator:

Kindness stood straight and walked Greed's way.

Greed:

Don't you dare.

Kindness:

We are 'The Promising Few'. Remember, kin?

Greed:

But we are not in Hazelton!

Kindness:

It should not matter, we took an oath.

We've made a promise, you and I both.

Narrator:

Greed looked around at his smiling brothers.

He sighed deeply and shrugged his shoulders.

Narrator:

The brothers grabbed bags from Strength's wagon.

They opened them up, and gave to the maiden:

A leg of a swine, a bottle of wine.

Two loaves of bread, and a scarf for her head.

Water in a canteen, a brick of cheese, and a small pouch of black beans.

Shoes for her feet, blankets for her sleep, and a sack of nuts and berries.

Kindness walked towards Greed. He stood up against him and held out a hand.

Greed looked down at Kindness's hand, and Greed had then maddened.

Greed:

Oh, no, no! She asked for something to eat.

She's not getting my money!

Kindness:

Greed…

Please?

Narrator:

Greed stared at Kindness's soft smile.

The more he stared, the more Kindness looked like their mother.

And although he hadn't seen her in a while,

He heard her speak to him, to "Do for others".

Greed grabbed his sack of gold,

He thought for a while, then shook his head *'no'*.

He put it back and grabbed two silvers.

Greed:

Here, this should do her.

Kindness:

Come on, Greed. A little more won't hurt.

We need to help her.

Greed:

UGH! KINDNESS! Here! That's it!

Narrator:

Greed gave him more silver bits.

Kindness placed the coins in a bag.

He then walked over to the ugly hag.

Kindness:

Here, this should do you some time.

Hag:

Uh…thank you! This is all fine.

The City of Hahm is past the grapevine.

But wait! Wait one second.

Who are you, gentlemen?

Kindness:

We are 'The Promising Few of Hazelton'.

Strength:

We work hard to build our names.

We help the poor and protect the lame.

Greed:

We have high profiles, notable reputations.

Brave:

We need not a witch, a God, nor even a vacation.

Greed:

We have smarts.

Strength:

Strength.

Kindness:

Hearts.

Brave:

And bravery.

Kindness:

And we will always help those in desperate need.

Hag:

No man has ever done at least half of what you just did.

And even if they did, they'd call me a bum.

You are some amazing men.

You truly are, I must repay some.

Kindness:

O, what makes a man is not only his actions, but the reason, purpose, and mostly the outcome.

We, 'The Promising Few', ask for nothing in return.

Just a simple thank you, and good luck on our journ'.

Hag:

What are your names?

Kindness:

They are Greed and Strength, I'm Kindness, he's Brave.

Hag:

Thank you, Kindness.

Kindness:

I wish you the best.

Strength:

If you don't mind, could you tell folks about us?

I am 'The Mighty Strength: Strongest Amongst'.

I can lift many barrels, a house if I must,

With only one hand. And the ladies lust.

Hag:

Uh…yes.

Narrator:

The hag packed her rewards and left.

Greed:

Hopefully she uses those berries to mask her stench.

Strength:

Or buy some perfume from a local bench.

Narrator:

Greed watched Kindness as they secured their items.

He glared and slightly frowned at him.

Greed:

Y'know, Kindness, ya shouldn't be so nice.

We'll be facing lots of obstacles, and you may be in our way.

Doing good for others comes with a price.

Thou will regret thy heart one day.

Kindness:

I think you're wrong there, Greed.

I'm as much help as you or Strength.

Being human is not being weak.

I may not contain a ferocious offence,

But what I am good at, is what you cannot resist.

I can do well on my own, and I'm not as dense

As you think or as you portray me to be.

You may think I do what people tell me,

But what you don't know is I do what's of Love and Creed.

Greed:

O? Thou can fend for himself?

Thou can do what thine pleases?

Thou can live without help?

No longer naive? Kindness deceives us.

Narrator:

Greed walked up to Kindness, cockily.

Greed:

O, my boots. Dost thou see?

They need some polishing.

Kindness, do so.

Narrator:

Kindness, in embarrassment, smiled and caressed his bow.

He thought for a long while before replying, so.

He started to examine Greed's red robe.

Kindness looked into his eyes and answered:

Kindness:

No.

Narrator:

Greed swept Kindness's legs, knocking him down on his back.

He looked down at him, drew his sword, and placed a foot on his chest.

He placed his sword under Kindness's chin and nicked his neck.

Strength:

O, Greed! Give it a rest!

Greed:

Now that you're down there, I think you can fulfil my request.

Yes?

Kindness:

Me being Kindness is not of weakness,

But you being Greed…even you digress.

Narrator:

Greed smiled deviously at Kindness, as if he proved his point.

He placed his sword into the sheath and pulled out a joint.

Brave helped Kindness back on his feet.

Kindness, scared, stared at Greed.

He watched him smoke on his herbal stick,

He mounted his horse and they continued their trip.

Maybe Greed was right, maybe Kindness was weak.

Or maybe Kindness was simply afraid of Greed.

Short in distance from the men was a grapevine in their views.

They saw taverns of drunken men and gallons of fine booze.

They looked over at ladies and broads, dancing arm and arm.

They walked through, a sign they saw. It read: *"City of Hahm"*.

Strength:

Look at all of this joy, brethren!

Greed:

Ah! This looks like heaven!

Kindness:

It looks like Sin City.

Brave:

Sicily?

Kindness:

Sin City.

Narrator:

They dismounted their horses and walked towards the fence.

In unison said Greed and Strength:

Greed and Strength:

WOMEN!

Narrator:

They saw the most beautiful broads.

It was as if they were painted by Gods.

They wasted no time introducing themselves

To the gorgeous women dressed in pastels.

Brave:

Strength, Greed!

Wait for me!

Narrator:

Kindness watched his aroused brothers

Coquet and browse for lovers.

Strength:

Hello ladies, I am The Mighty Strength,

The prettiest of gents.

Look, watch this!

Narrator:

Strength rushed over to a wagon of melons,

He lifted it to the sky with the brightest grin.

In amazement, the ladies were yellin'.

Their jaws dropped and their eyes widened.

Woman 1:

O my! You're very strong!

Strength:

I bet no man can do this in the City of Hahm.

Greed:

I am The Handsome Greed.

And as you can see, my money speaks.

Narrator:

Greed pulls out his hefty bag of silver coins.

He shakes it around to hear its noise.

The ladies whisper and snicker together.

They were eager to swindle the rich brother.

Greed:

Besides my richness, I have the smarts.

I created maths, science, tools, and arts.

Woman 2:

What about you?

What do you do?

Brave:

Me? I'm Brave.

I'm never afraid!

I've fought lions, bears, sharks, and snakes!

Some of those battles they say I lost.

But being fearless was worth the cost.

Woman 3:

And he, back there, what's his purpose?

Strength:

Oh, he is simply Kindness.

He councils couples for divorces and such.

He and Greed gives advice, much.

But don't ever try to toy with he.

He's married and won't commit adultery.

Woman 1:

Where are you from, fine gentlemen?

Brave:

We come from Hazelton, on an important mission.

Greed:

We are 'The Promising Few', descendants from the well-known Love and Creed.

Woman 2:

O! The creators of lands and realities?

I didn't know that they had children!

Woman 3:

These aren't children, honey. These are men!

And blessed with the greatest abilities.

Woman 1:

They are Gods if you ask me.

Woman 2:

Well, don't you boys want to join us for a while?

I'm sure you're tired from travelling miles.

Narrator:

The feverish brothers followed the ladies into the tavern,

While Kindness went on a small tour without them.

He examined the city of well beings.

Some were singing, some were cleaning.

The city smelled fresh of apples and pine.

The buildings were painted brown and white.

The citizens of Hahm sold goods and clothes.

Kindness bought his brothers some clothes for the roads.

The concrete was lavender with weeds around.

The sky was pink, and orange were the clouds.

A fountain was placed in the middle of the city.

Where children made wishes and tossed in their shillings.

The citizens were well dressed, rich and dandy,

In hats, jewels, and laced panties.

Kindness stopped by a small workshop

Where a few men were welding a prop.

The men had beards longer than time,

Red and curly, thick like vines.

Bald they were, their heads did shine.

Tall and muscular, but fat like swine.

Kindness:

Excuse me, men,

I have a question.

What is it that you are weldin'?

Blacksmith 1:

Well, right now, we're making an axe.

We have other work in the backs.

Kindness:

May I take a look? I'm willing to buy.

Blacksmith 1:

Of course you can! Follow my guy.

Narrator:

Kindness followed a blacksmith into the shacks.

There, he saw dozens of artefacts.

He saw the shiniest swords, shields, and sacks.

He saw zings and things that zip and zap.

He saw hammers and helmets, and knicks n' knacks.

He saw fixtures and things that flip and flap.

He saw boots and loots, and this and that.

He saw a case, a brace, a mace, an axe,

A disk, a flisk, a flask, a mask,

A back, a pack, a tisk, a task.

He saw things that push and things that pull,

Things the cush and things that cull.

He saw things that buckle and things that knuckle.

He saw feathery things that make you chuckle.

He saw things that zoom and things that vroom,

And things that light an entire room.

He saw things that clip and things that clap.

He saw things that rip and things that wrap.

He saw things that tip and things that tap.

He saw things that whip and things that whack.

He saw things that dive and things that fly,

And things you shoot up in the sky.

He saw things that hook and things that cook,

Things that bob and things that lob,

Things that prick, things that prack,

Things that lick and things that lack.

He saw things that strip and things that strap,

Things that flick and things that flack,

Things that kick and things that crack,

Things that drip and things that drap.

He saw things that drift and things that draft,

Things that lift and things that latch,

Things that knock and things that rock,

Things that pop and things that bop.

He saw things that mitch and things that match,

Things that pitch and things that patch.

He saw things that fist and things that fast,

Things that mist and things that mast.

He saw things that tilt, things that spill,

Things that turn, things that burn,

Things that wish, things that wash,

Things he thought were pish and posh.

He saw things that bing and things that bang,

Things that sing, things that sang,

Things that ring, things that wrang,

He saw a blackened boomerang.

Out of all those things that Kindness saw,

Only one thing left him in awe.

Back at the tavern, Greed examined.

He saw men hauling barrels of beer.

He sat down his glass and quickly chimed in,

To solve the problem that had appeared.

Greed:

Y'know, you shouldn't store beer in barrels. They should only be placed in barrels once ready to dispense.

It will sour quickly, within minutes!

Try storing your new brews in the cooler in tins.

Brewer:

You believe it keeps it fresh, friend?

Greed:

Absolutely, and it keeps the supplies on rotation.

And jot down the dates for expiration.

Down in Hazelton, we only brew on day thirty.

It saves us time, energy, and of course, money!

Brewer:

Say, you're pretty smart. Who dost thou be?

Greed:

I am The Handsome Greed.

Brewer:

Do you think you can help us make tins for our brewing's?

Greed:

Sure, I'll help ya…for a fee.

Narrator:

Brave entered the tavern and interrupted Greed.

Overwhelmed but happy, he seemed.

Brave:

Greed! Greed! Greed!

We need your money!

The fellas are having a tournament.

A fight of the local and strongest men.

I have entered and so have Strength.

And I have a feeling we're going to win!

Narrator:

Greed dug into his pouch of gold.

He placed some in Brave's hands to hold.

Greed:

Here, bet my money only on Strength.

And when I win, bring me my profits!

Narrator:

Brave ran off to the back of the pub,

With joy and gold within his gloves.

He walked up to the tournament host

And bet on Strength, five thousand golds.

He walked over to Strength's corner,

He leaned over his enormous shoulders.

Brave:

Greed gave us gold for us to bet.

When you're done, I'm up next!

Narrator:

Strength waited patiently in his corner,

Then out the other entered a man in armour.

His gear shimmered across their faces.

He held his sword high as they watched his paces.

The host of the tourney stood high at his desk,

He asked for attention as he introduced the guest.

Host:

Ladies and gentlemen let's continue this feature!

I do see we have new contenders.

To your right, to start this event,

With golden hair and a chiselled chin,

He surely is one handsome man.

Rise from the stands and clap your hands,

For The Mighty Strength of Hazelton!

Narrator:

Strength flexed his muscles as the audience booed.

Strength grinned at their hateful buzz.

The locals didn't know of this mighty dude.

They had no idea how strong he was.

Host:

And now, to your left, your favourite warrior.

With a winning streak of forty-four,

Cheer for Hahm's very own,

Sir Thaddeus-Marius McAnus Lowe!

Brave:

Haha! Anus.

Narrator:

The locals cheered for Thaddeus-Marius.

He and Strength stood in the centre,

Waiting for the host to cue the fight.

Strength looked down at the well-known winner.

He smiled arrogantly at the armoured knight.

The fight began, and the knight drew his sword.

He swung it vigorously at The Mighty Strength.

Strength caught it and the crowd roared.

They then silenced, the sword was bent.

Strength grabbed Sir Lowe, swung him 'round and 'round.

He then let go, and Lowe flew out of town.

His body left a hole in the ceiling.

The locals had an enraged feeling.

Strength dusted his hands and looked towards the stands.

Strength:

Who is my next man?

Narrator:

Some of the folks cheered, they were greatly amused.

The bettors threw fits, they had thousands to lose.

To the host's desk, Brave went in a scramble.

He collected the money he won in the gamble.

He went back to Strength, who had a plan.

The Gambler's Room, he started to scan.

Strength:

Brave, look. Do you see those men over here?

Brave:

Yes, well dressed. I do see.

Strength:

Those must be the high bidders.

They placed a bet but had no idea I'd succeed.

Now, you're next.

And since you're my brother, it's you they will bet.

Since I'm strong, they'll think you, too, are the best.

But what they don't know is, you won't win.

So, I won't bet money on you at this event.

They'll lose for sure and we'll win thousands!

Brave:

O, Strength! You're sneaky! Tricky!

Strength:

Yes, indeed.

Narrator:

At the blacksmith's shop, Kindness picked up a grappling hook.

He admired its nooks and fingered its crooks.

It was something he had never seen before,

Something Greed hadn't invented yet.

He dropped its black rope onto the floor,

He saw his reflection in the silver neck.

He fell in love with the beautiful invention.

He felt he would need the new creation.

Kindness:

What is this strange object?

Blacksmith 2:

A grappling hook. Ya like it?

Kindness:

Yes. What can I buy it for?

Blacksmith 2:

Eighteen hundred forty-four.

Kindness:

Silver?

Blacksmith 2:

Gold.

Kindness:

O…

Will you hold it for me? I have to talk to my brother.

Blacksmith 2:

Sure.

Narrator:

Kindness sat the grappling hook down

And travelled back through the lovely town.

The tavern was packed with drunken men.

The air was filled with must and sin.

Kindness entered, shy and sweetly,

In search of his older brother, Greed.

He found Greed, coddled by women,

Feeding him grapes, bread, and lemon.

Kindness made his way through the reeking crowd.

He came up to Greed and spoke aloud.

Kindness:

Greed,

I'm in need of money.

Greed:

Kindness, Kindness.

Sit down, take a rest.

Woman 1:

We've heard so much about you, Kindness.

Woman 2:

And how one of you will be a royal highness.

Kindness:

Yes, yes.

Excuse me, miss.

Greed,

I need to speak with thee.

Woman 1:

So, Kindness, if you become king,

What will you do with your royalties?

Kindness:

Provide for my family and then my city.

Woman 3:

Your wife is a very lucky woman. It's sad she's not here to celebrate.

Kindness:

Well, we're not here to celebrate, we're here to take a small break.

Woman 2:

Your wife's absence was a terrible mistake.

Narrator:

The woman caressed Kindness' face.

Kindness:

Yeah, anyway…

Narrator:

Kindness pushed her away.

Narrator:

A staggering man bumped into Kindness.

Kindness turned and spilt the man's beer.

Drunken Man:

Watch it lackey! You did that on purpose!

Kindness:

I'm sorry, sir, I didn't see you here.

Don't worry, my brother will buy you a beer.

Narrator:

Greed, out of anger, spat out his beer.

He grabbed Kindness by his ear.

He pulled him and placed him against a wall.

Greed's breath reeked of alcohol.

Greed:

What's up kid?

Huh? Ya stupid!?

Ya mind telling me what you're doin'?

Kindness:

Well, I didn't want to fight the man, even you couldn't handle him.

But now that I've gotten your attention,

I need you to listen.

I…uh…I need,

Some…shimmering,

Sterling,

Things.

Narrator:

Kindness was scared to ask Greed,

Once again, for his money.

Greed stared at Kindness, blankly.

He was too buzzed to even think.

Greed:

What?

Kindness:

I need the beautiful loots…the treasures,

Of pleasures…

I need…the 'ments, or mints.

The bling.

The cha-ching, things…

Greed:

Are you asking me for money?

Kindness:

Uh, yes. Please.

Greed:

No.

Kindness:

But, Greed!

Greed:

You offered me to pay a man a beer for free.

You gave my money to a hag for free.

I'm not lending any more of MY money!

Kindness:

Oh, so you rather the hag to offer you pleasures for money?

Narrator:

Kindness joked, laughed, and smirked.

Greed:

You are one disgusting jerk.

Kindness:

Greed, please. It was a joke. You didn't have a problem paying those courtesans.

Greed:

No, I didn't give them one cent.

Kindness:

Greed, I'm your sibling.

You shouldn't have a problem helping me.

A local blacksmith has something we need.

I need to buy it for our journey.

Narrator:

Greed sighed, for once again.

Kindness's eyes gave him in

Greed:

How much is he asking for?

Kindness:

Eighteen hundred forty-four.

Greed:

Silver?

Kindness:

Gold.

Greed:

O, HEAVEN'S NO!

Whatever it is, we can do without!

Narrator:

Greed went back to his velvet couch.

Kindness had a strong feeling that they needed the hook,

And he was going to get it, no matter what it took.

He decided to return to the blacksmith,

And gain the hook by using his gift.

Brave and Strength finished several rounds.

Strength won many, Brave won none.

The audience made indistinctive sounds.

The bidders were heavily worrisome.

No matter what opponent the host threw his way,

Strength was unbeatable and prosperous that day.

He smashed his opponents into the walls.

He jumped higher than mountains and ran faster than cheetahs.

And if his opponents were wearing drawers,

He made them ruin it with their own excreta.

The people of Hahm feared Strength.

There was no way they could beat him.

Though the audience was in amazement,

The gamblers were ragin'.

Strength had fun, he toyed with the fighters.

With a big grin, he showed he was mightier.

He buried them, carried them. The host, he harried him.

He flaunted for the women who wanted to marry him.

Some of the fighters successfully injured him,

But it was Strength who stood tall in the end.

The Hahm locals were no match for The Mighty Strength.

He was always destined to win.

Strength:

Brave, here's the plan for this last fight.

I will bet it all on you!

Brave:

But, Strength, I haven't won one time!

Strength:

That's the idea. Here's what we'll do,

The bidders won't bet on you since you lose.

But, we will cheat and make you win.

I will assist you with my mighty wind.

Narrator:

Brave entered the match, happy and fearless!

It was the final match held that evening.

Brave decided to battle gearless.

Strength noticed the high bidders happily bidding.

Brave's opponent was a well fit man.

He wore nothing but a brown kilt and his body was tan.

The man growled as the final match began.

He swung the club he had in his hand.

Brave jumped around and circled the man,

And from behind the pillar, Strength blew his wind.

The man also spun around,

Becoming dizzy before falling to the ground.

The audience watched as Brave circled the fighter.

They, too, became dizzy and felt a bit lighter.

They wondered if Brave was as strong as Strength.

They watched as his runs made vicious winds.

No one knew Strength was blowing the man,

Deceiving the host and the people in the stands.

The wind was so strong, it lifted the man

Up from the ground and into the air.

The man flew over and fell in the stands.

Out of disbelief, the host rose from his chair.

The host checked on the man and he had concluded

That Brave had beaten the final opponent.

The audience cheered in utter amusement.

The bidders threw fits in the scandalous moment.

Brave ran to the hosts desk to collect his funds.

Three million shillings they had won.

The host grabbed his wrist and pinned him against a wall.

Brave looked up at the man, who was angry and tall.

Host:

You boys got nerve coming here to cheat.

You're nothing but low lives from the street.

Brave and Strength from Hazelton,

I oughta show ya how to fight a real man!

Narrator:

Strength placed his hand on the host's shoulder.

Strength:

Remove your hand from my brother.

Host:

Or else what, 'The Mighty Strength'?

You're gonna blow me with your death wind?

Narrator:

And Strength did.

The host flew away like a boneless dummy.

The brothers then, happily, collected their money.

Kindness arrived at the blacksmith's shoppe.

He cleared his throat before he talked.

Kindness:

Excuse me.

Blacksmith 1:

He's back, O!

Blacksmith 2:

You got the money?

Kindness:

Yes. Well, no.

Um, I was hoping we could bargain?

Blacksmith 2:

Well…it depends.

Kindness:

Would you sell it to me for five hundred bits?

Blacksmith 2:

This grappling hook is worth more than this.

What about that?

On your back?

I can do a trade, y'know.

Kindness:

No.

I mean, my mother made me this bow.

It's sentimental.

Blacksmith 1:

And you arriving with low money is accidental?

Kindness:

Look, my brothers and I are on an important mission.

And I believe this will be an excellent assist.

I do not have funds, but I will return it,

If you loan it to me for this one trip.

Blacksmith 2:

Aye, I'm sure you're a good kid.

But I'm sorry, I can't just give you this.

Narrator:

The blacksmiths turned Kindness away.

His glory gift was no use that day.

He rode his horse back to the stuffy pub,

Wondering why he had such bad luck.

Was his only strength his true weakness?

Or did he fail because of human cheapness?

He stopped his horse and had a plan.

If kindness couldn't sway them, maybe a fabulist can.

Kindness:

We have to go over the mountains to save our mother!

I just want one more chance to hold her.

She's ill, very ill.

We promised to visit her Ville.

We won't be able to cross the mountains without the use of this hook.

But if you still won't let me have it, just let her know how much it took,

How many days it took, how many nights it took, how much begging it took for us to get a chance to see her.

Will you travel the mountains for me and let her know that we tried and we were desperately eager?

Go! Tell her! Tell her about our procedures!

Tell her before her life gets taken by an incurable seizure!

Blacksmith 2:

Okay kid! Okay!

Here, it's yours to take.

Kindness:

O, thank you! My mother's been saved.

I'll return it in a few days.

Narrator:

Kindness mounted his horse and rode back to the tavern.

He grinned widely, for his plan had worked.

Brave and Strength sat next to Greed.

They handed him their earned money.

Greed:

O, sweet heavens! You boys have done it!

Look at my money, it's perfect.

Brave:

I didn't win, but Strength did of course.

Look at this money, we must rejoice!

Strength:

Don't be silly, Brave! You won the last match!

Now the ladies think you're a catch.

But of course I did the heavy work.

And I did it all with my famous smirk.

O, I'm so great!

I'm heaven made!

No one can defeat Strength…

Brave:

Nor Brave!

Greed:

Here you boys go, two shillings apiece.

You boys earned it, don't spend it all in one place.

Strength:

Say, what can you do about our wounds?

Greed:

A few garlic cloves, that should do.

Narrator:

After patching up his brothers wounds,

They drank and partied to jolly tunes.

All through the night, the three brothers fornicated.

They danced and smoked and celebrated.

Until the a.m., the brothers had fun.

In the afternoon, they woke up hung.

The tavern was clean but it still smelled foul.

When the brothers woke up, no one was found.

Strength:

Greed, Brave. Wake up.

We're the only ones left in this pub.

Brave:

What day is it?

Strength:

The day we continue our trip.

I fear we've overslept.

Greed:

Oh no, no, no, no, no, no, no!

My silvers! They're gone! Those dirty hoes!

Strength:

It's alright, Greed.

We have all we need.

Brave:

Did they take our money from the tourney!?

Greed:

No, I hid those winnings.

Narrator:

The brothers left the tavern in a bloody mess.

Their hair was all over, and stale were their breaths.

They stumbled and staggered in sloppy steps,

They stretched their backs and cracked their necks.

They exited the tavern and met up with Kindness.

He was feeding their horses and adjusting their harness.

Kindness:

Good morning, miscreants.

Greed:

We don't have time for your ignorance,

Or your, "You're all sinners," and foolishness.

We already know your innocence.

Kindness:

It was a joke.

I am ready to go.

Strength:

Yes, we know.

Narrator:

The brothers continued their trip on the lavender road.

Scene III. Swallowing Swamp

Narrator:

The Few ate their meals of bread and beans as they continued their journey to the Sucrex Cave.

Greed gave his corn to his midnight horse and carried a convo with his brother, Brave.

Greed:

Learn how to control your trusty steed.

You're swerving and you nearly bumped me.

Guide your horse, don't let it guide thee.

It's time you learn something from me.

Brave:

O, thanks! But I didn't ask you, Greed.

Greed:

You don't need to ask; I've eyes that see.

You are sloppy, insubordinate, and foolhardy.

You are not fit to be a king.

Brave:

There's no need for jealousy.

Greed:

Trust me, there is not a thing about you that I envy.

Narrator:

As the two brothers had their conversation, Kindness and Strength had one of their own.

They whispered softly behind Greed and Brave as they guided their horses down the road.

Strength:

Kindness, what's wrong? You look down again.

Kindness:

I was just thinking about how I'm not…a man.

I turned down Hazelton. I'm always hesitant.

And for myself, I cannot stand.

I just feel like I would make a terrible king.

I've got as much hope as a stray string.

Narrator:

Strength listened to Kindness's dispirited remarks.

So, he presented him with facts to change his heart.

Strength:

Kindness, let me tell you something you may not understand.

Our parents were always one thousand steps ahead.

They knew what was needed and created all things: plants and man.

They are not to be questioned, debated, or disrespected.

Whatever our parents say, goes:

Green beeth the grass, red beeth the rose.

Women beareth children, and children groweth old.

Summer carries the heat, and winter bringeth the cold.

So, when our parents wrote in their will for the winner to become royalty,

You won Kindness, and you are our rightful King.

It is not to be argued with, not to be contemplated.

You are our majesty, thus, fated.

We cannot change our fate, we can only live it.

It will all pass muster at the end of this mission.

Narrator:

Kindness had a surprised look on his face, as if he had solved an impossible quiz.

After hearing Strength say, "What our parents say, goes", their whole adventure started to make sense.

Greed:

What are you two whispering about back there?

Strength:

O, we've just noticed you're losing hair!

Narrator:

Kindness and Brave giggled at the pun.

Greed became irritated by their childish fun.

Brave:

You're getting a bit old here, Greed.

Strength:

He's balding!

Greed:

And you're only a year younger than me!

You're well on your way, Mr. Strong.

Narrator:

Greed pulled his horse up to a pond.

He looked at his reflection and saw their tale.

Greed:

Lying to me won't do any of you well.

Just say you wish you were as handsome as me.

Brave:

Yes, I wish I were The Handsome Greed.

No, but I wish I had some of your ladies.

Greed:

Speaking of ladies, the whores of Hahm must pay me!

But I'll excuse them since they are rare beauties.

Say, Strength, Hazelton doesn't have any pretty broads.

Strength:

If that's so, then why have you slept with them all?

Greed:

A man can only wait so long.

Brave:

He hasn't been with all the women in Hazelton. What about Kindness' wife?

Greed:

She was never my type.

She's a problem I call venereal.

Not even our parents saw her as wife material.

Kindness:

You can joke about whatever.

Humiliate my wife, you will never.

Greed:

She humiliated herself when she stepped out on you.

Kindness:

And forgiveness is the reason why our marriage grew.

Strength:

It was a tough time for you, Kindness, I remember.

You were crying at my post that December.

And Priscilla, she's beautiful of course.

But I'm not sure she's even yours.

Kindness:

Priscilla favours her mother as Pete favours me.

You shouldn't worry about my wife's past when Greed has many after he.

Brave:

Maybe that's why he's so greedy,

He's saving up money for his offspring's.

Greed:

Those rascals are not mine!

Unlike most men, I withdraw on time.

Narrator:

They continued to laugh and joke about Greed,

Within seconds, they felt a swift breeze.

The horses stopped at a dark blue lake.

The sky had mysteriously turned green and grey.

They tried nudging the horses to move, but they would not budge.

The horses refused to walk through what seemed to be black mud.

The air was filled with burning rubber.

The lake made sounds: *flubber, blubber.*

Brave stepped into the substance with a *clomp, clomp.*

Greed:

I believe we have reached the Swallowing Swamp.

Narrator:

They examined the swamp and its gloomy surroundings.

They could not bear the gruesome soundings.

Lost boots and boats were across the scenes.

Naked and black were the hollow trees.

The grass was brown, engulfed in tar.

They saw skeleton bones floating afar.

The bitterness of the rubber filled their lungs.

They swore they could taste it upon their tongues.

A crow swooped by and cawed loudly.

It alarmed The Few and cursed the team.

They dismounted their horses to thoroughly observe

The next curb they had been served.

Kindness clomped into the swamp to assist Brave.

He looked towards the hollow trees and saw a stave.

Kindness:

Brave, pick up your feet.

Brave:

I can't, they're down deep.

Kindness:

That wooden shaft, try to reach.

Brave:

I'm trying. I can't. See?

Narrator:

While still examining the sombre course,

Greed walked up to the swamp and stood at the brim.

His feet began to sink with an uncanny force.

The swamp was alive and pulling him in.

He held up his fist to stop Strength at his horse.

Strength:

Come on, girl. Come on.

Greed:

Strength, they're not coming in.

Strength:

What's wrong?

The wind?

Greed:

Cunning, the witch.

This place, these trips, it's all a trick.

This swamp is alive, it's pulling us in.

It will tear the flesh off of our skin.

People have died here, this swamp ate.

But I trust our craftsman, our boots should keep us safe.

Narrator:

Greed looked over at Kindness and Brave.

Greed:

You two, stop moving.

You're slowly sinking.

Brave:

Help us, Greed!

Greed:

I'm thinking, I'm thinking.

Kindness:

We're going to die, we're on the brink!

Greed:

Settle down, you won't die. I told you; I'm thinking.

Narrator:

Greed looked down at his sinking feet.

The only way out of the swamp was a possible death.

He squinted his eyes and clenched his teeth.

In the cool yellow wind, he saw his breath.

Strength gathered the horses and held them high up.

His body was stiff, his hands were cupped.

He jumped into the swamp and stomped his way through.

Wonkily walking, he lost their food.

The gooey water flew up and covered his siblings.

The goo went into Greed's ear, blocking his hearing.

Greed:

STRENGTH STOP! YOU'RE MAKING IT WORSE!

Narrator:

Out of desperate anger, Greed had cursed.

Brave:

Our food, Strength, you've lost our feed!

Kindness:

Forget the food; get us out of here, Greed!

Strength:

What should I do, Greed?

Greed:

I'm trying to think!

Narrator:

Greed could barely hear his crying brothers.

His heart was aching from seeing them suffer.

His hearing was muffled, his brain was foggy.

He felt the tension rising in his body.

It was like, for the first time, he didn't know what to do.

He looked up to the sky and in his view,

The grey clouds covered the entire sky.

He heard the roaring thunder passing by.

Lightning struck and blinded his eyes.

The rain poured down, and the swamp did rise.

Greed's vision became blurry as he looked around.

He saw a shadow peeking out from between the trees.

He saw to his right, his brothers who almost drowned.

He bent over and grabbed his aching knees.

He looked to his left at Strength struggling

To contain the horses upon his shoulders.

Strength's body, to Greed, was doubling.

He finally told him his only plan to get them over.

Greed:

The only way across, is simply across.

It is us you must toss.

Strength:

That's a long way to the other side!

If I do that, you all will die!

Narrator:

Greed didn't hear a word Strength said.

His body and voice became weak and dead.

Strength:

Greed, I can't hold on to our steed.

They're becoming rowdy.

Brave:

Help us, Greed!

Kindness:

We're sinking!

Strength:

What do you need of me?

Narrator:

Their voices were mute.

Greed was confused.

He looked up at the sky while still holding his knees.

The sun barely peeked from behind the trees.

After seeing the sun, his sight was gone and

Everything turned white, then Greed had fallen.

Black.

From white to black, quickly like a zap.

His eyes closed and sight, he lacked.

Black.

He scarcely heard the rain and thunder, coming in and out.

They were going to die in the swamp, no doubt.

Greed woke up lying face down on top of a cliff.

He had trouble opening his eyes. But once he did,

He saw nothing but a beautiful blue sky with white clouds.

There was nothing. Not a mountain, not a tree, not a sound.

He felt a hand caress his neck.

He raised his head and looked to his left.

His vision was blurred from the sun above.

But after a moment, he saw his mother, Love.

His eyes focused on her warming smirk.

She wore a green tunic with a matching skirt.

Her eyes twinkled with beguiling brightness.

Her hair slightly curled just like Kindness'.

Greed placed his hand upon her chin.

With his thumb, he felt her lips and skin.

Greed:

I can feel you.

Love:

Me too.

Greed:

Are you a ghost?

Love:

No.

Greed:

Am I dead?

Love:

Yes.

Narrator:

Love grinned as Greed became anxious.

Love:

It was a joke. You're just unconscious.

Greed:

I'm not sure. This looks like heaven.

Love:

You really think *you* would make it into heaven?

Narrator:

Greed frowned at his mother's question.

Love:

It was another joke, relax my dear.

Come closer, come here.

I decided to take this time to talk to you.

That was a frightening scene down there.

Your brothers are struggling to get through the swamp, love.

Even your father, he couldn't bear

Watching you struggle from up above.

I wonder who's going to save you

From the sinking swallowing swamp of goo…

Greed, look at me. I love you.

Greed:

WHY!? After all I've done!?

Love:

You are still my son.

And I trust you to wake up and protect my other kids.

Greed:

You mean protect Kindness.

Love:

O, jealousy blocks one from succeeding,

And you know that, Greed.

Besides, you are my first love.

And when first comes…

Greed and Love:

Nothing surpasses thereof.

Greed:

…Where is he?

Love:

Your father? I believe he's…

Greed:

Burning in hell? Paying his price?

Love:

He decided to take my advice.

And that's to let me handle you.

Greed:

You couldn't even handle the truth,

When you found out who he really was.

You stood behind him, though he broke your trust.

Love:

Greed, I'm not here to talk about your father's past,

I'm here to talk about the future thou hast.

And to wake you up to be there for Kindness…

Greed:

Kindness that, Kindness this.

God damn that useless kid!

Love:

To be there for Kindness, Brave, and Strength…

And Hazelton.

Greed:

Tell me something. Why do we have these great gifts, yet we're still cursed?

Why am I greedy? Why is your baby naive? Why is Brave dumb? Why is Strength egotistic?

Love:

No spell can ever or will ever be reversed.

There's a price to pay for what the witches emit.

Greed:

So, it is true. You were infertile and turned to a witch.

Love:

After all the stories I've told you, you should know this.

Greed:

In the scriptures your husband writes about, infertility is a fair bequest.

And those who alter their fate with black magic shall receive death.

And so does thou who holds the gift.

That's you, dad, all of your kids!

Love:

You cannot change your fate; you can only live it.

I sense you do not want to hear from me.

So, I'll send you back, Greed.

Narrator:

Love touched Greed's knees.

Once again, they started aching.

Greed fell flat on his face.

He felt pain, his heart started to race.

Love looked down into Greed's eyes.

And just like before, Greed went blind.

Love:

I love you, Greed.

Narrator:

Love whispered to Greed.

He opened his mouth but couldn't speak.

Love:

Greed. Wake up!

Wake up, Greed.

Wake up!

Wake up!

Kindness:

Wake up, Greed!

Greed, wake up!

Wake up!

Greed!

Narrator:

Greed opened his eyes and looking down at him,

Was Kindness, screaming his name like a hymn.

Greed's vision slowly became clear.

He removed the goo from his ear.

He rose up slowly, aching in pain.

Though it had stopped, he could smell the rain.

He looked over at his brother, Strength.

He was unharmed and fixing the wagon.

Greed:

What happened?

Strength:

I did what you said.

I threw the horses over.

I threw Brave over.

I threw Kindness over.

Kindness landed on top of Brave,

So, he missed the pave'.

He's safe.

Greed:

Yay…

And what about you?

Strength:

I stomped my way through.

Narrator:

Greed stood up and walked towards his horse.

He reached down and grabbed his purse.

Greed:

Forget the wagon.

Help me apply this medicine.

Kindness:

I bought us garments while we were in Hahm.

When we get washed, we can try them on.

Strength:

Thank you, Kindness. Greed, our horses aren't breathing.

I felt them, their bodies are freezing.

Greed:

We'll just have to go without.

We can't stop now.

Narrator:

Greed reached in his bag for cannabis.

He walked over and handed it to Kindness.

Greed:

When Brave wakes up, give him this.

Light it, he's supposed to smoke it.

Narrator:

Kindness palmed the medicine and looked into Greed's eyes.

He felt his stare getting colder and colder.

Greed walked away and examined the skies.

He grabbed his robe and threw it over his shoulder.

Scene **IV**. Hot Springs

Narrator:

After healing from their swamp battle,

The Few removed their bags from their deceased mares.

Kindness kissed his horses saddle,

And groomed its dirty white hair.

They walked through the sprouting woods,

Continuing their quest and hunting for goods.

The trees were tall and very healthy.

It looked as if it were the season of spring.

There was a dirt trail they decided to course,

Hoping it would lead them to a useful source.

Kindness:

What drug did you give Brave? He's walking wonkily.

Greed:

Mariauna is not a drug. Think of it as broccoli.

Green, healthy, and something you need.

It's for relaxation and his joint pain.

Brave must've had too much, but it's no worry.

It'll wear off throughout the day.

Strength:

His walk does not differ from any other day.

Staggering, falling, and always in the way.

Narrator:

They continued and stumbled through the woods of beauty.

They walked and walked for almost eternity.

Although it looked as if the woods were nourishing,

Not one fruit or animal could be seen.

They looked but only saw brown and green,

Dirt, grass, and lofty trees.

There wasn't a bird to chirp or tweet.

There wasn't a hare for them to eat.

There wasn't a pond to wet their feet.

There wasn't a person for them to meet.

Their feet ached and became very sore.

Their necks were stiff, and their postures were poor.

The sun burned the backs of the four.

They felt like they were losing a war.

Brave stopped and fell to the ground.

He panted and sweated and groaned like a hound.

His brother's, too, stopped and gathered around.

They each were unsightly unsound.

Strength:

These woods, it's like they never end.

Kindness:

How much longer 'til our destination?

Greed:

Quit crying and let us go!

It takes longer if you keep walking slow.

Brave:

I don't know.

Kindness:

We really need a break.

Strength:

My skin is dry, it's starting to flake.

My beauty is fading.

Greed:

And I'm tired of waiting!

Brave:

What is that between the trees?

Kindness:

I think Brave sees something.

Greed:

He's just hallucinating.

Kindness:

No, there, see?

Strength:

What is that, yo?

Greed:

I don't know.

Kindness:

I think it's mist…or maybe fog?

Strength:

No, it's smoke.

Kindness:

It can't be, it's no choking smog.

Narrator:

Greed drew his sword and walked slowly towards the mysterious smoke.

He led his brothers carefully past the trees of oak.

He hid behind his shield as Kindness helped Brave up from the ground.

The closer they got to the fog, they heard splashing and blobbing sounds.

Greed held his sword high, ready to defeat whatever was behind the mossy tree.

He turned to face behind the tree, and brightly, the sun beamed.

Greed:

It's steam. This is a spring.

These- these are hot springs!

Narrator:

They watched the geysers with deep concentration.

And in their eyes was exhilaration.

Greed:

O, our parents would tell us about this location.

Now it's no longer in our imagination!

Strength:

Look at its profound beauty!

It's almost as beautiful as me.

Narrator:

The geysers boiled and bubbled wildly.

The brothers smiled and frolicked childly.

The water did burst high into the sky.

It cleaned their skin but burnt their eyes.

But the longing brothers paid it no mind.

They began to walk around for something to find.

The brothers stopped at a bubbling pool.

The brothers then began to drool.

Without a thought, they started to undress.

They jumped in, leaving behind Kindness.

Greed:

Aahh, this feels magnificent.

Brave:

I love the way the bubbles tickle my skin.

Strength:

Kindness don't be shy. Come on in.

Narrator:

Kindness removed his bow and arrow shyly.

He unbuttoned his top and tossed it down.

His older brothers watched him, slyly.

He took off his boots and left them on the ground.

He saw the look on their faces as he stood up straight.

Not once did they turn their eyes away.

Kindness pulled down his bottoms as his brothers continued to stare.

Strength:

Whoa ho ho! Sir Cock-a-Lot! A pocket sparrow with plums to pair!

Greed:

I see why your wife cheated, kid. It's pretty sad down there.

Brave:

No wonder he's so nice, Greed.

He has no choice but to be!

Narrator:

Kindness joined his brothers in the hot springs.

He was embarrassed but not quite angry.

Kindness:

A little small, I agree, yes.

But I'm not the one suffering from impotence.

Greed:

O, there's nothing unable about my body.

Ask Morena, Wendy, Sella, or Tahdi.

Strength:

So, you are the father of Sella's son?

Greed:

Only in her dreams, that wild one.

Narrator:

They bathed and laughed and joked in the pool.

The weather began to get a bit cool.

Brave yawned and his stomach rumbled.

He looked around and softly mumbled.

Brave:

I'm hungry, can we look for food?

Greed:

Not until I'm in the mood.

Strength:

Come on, Greed, we've had enough relaxation.

I'm starting to suffer from dehydration.

Kindness:

I bought us clothes from The City of Hahm.

Here, take it. Try them on.

Narrator:

Kindness gave his older brothers their clothing.

They put them on and admired the sewing's.

For Greed, all black, from head to toe.

A button up top, a belt and buckle.

His buckle and heels of his new boots were silver to match his shield and sword.

He admired his gifts from his younger brother and stood tall as if he were a lord.

For strength, a fitted golden suit,

A purple vest, and purple boots.

A purple kilt for his curvy waist,

A golden helmet to shield his face.

For brave a caramel laced sweater,

A rope with tassels to hold his pants together.

Caramel bottoms, and mocha clogs.

Mocha gloves outlined in bronze.

And for himself, Kindness wore white.

Made of cotton, what caressed him tight,

Was a long-sleeved shirt that covered his neck.

His pants were so tight, it enhanced his assets.

Satin silver buttons lined down his chest.

He placed a silver pendant on his left breast.

Silver laces were tightened on his loafers,

And metal plates rested on his shoulders.

The plates held a white cape,

Which helped define his petite shape.

Greed washed the goo from his red coat,

He put it on and began to gloat.

Greed:

My looks are of fineness.

Thank you, Kindness.

Strength:

I don't like how my beauty is hidden.

But if this is real gold, you are forgiven.

Kindness:

O, Strength, it is for protection.

A face that is pretty must stay in good condition.

Strength:

I agree.

Brave:

Can we now look for feed?

Narrator:

The brothers went separate ways to search for food for their journey.

They climbed the trees and ran through the woods in a hurry.

They searched high and low and behind the shrubs,

But they couldn't find any decent grubs.

Greed had found a berry bush and he examined it.

The strange berries were dark with blackened stems.

Greed:

Deadly Nightshade, inedible,

But useful.

Narrator:

Greed pocketed the poisonous berry and continued searching for edibles.

Kindness perched high in a tree, foraging for animals.

He waited and waited, but nothing passed him by.

He became upset and released a sigh.

Within minutes he heard a sneeze.

He turned around and sat on his knees.

There, in the woods, in the gentle breeze,

A doe was sniffing, surrounded by bees.

A smile lit up on Kindness' face.

He got on one knee, his heart started to race.

He reached to his back and pulled an arrow from his quiver.

He placed the arrow on the string of his bow and felt a jitter.

He stared at the doe, breathing slowly from his nose.

He aimed for its skull as she sniffed on a rose.

As he aimed for the doe, he had a hazy memory.

He, as a child, aimed a slingshot carefully.

His mother stood behind him and watched him play.

Love:

Don't let distractions get in your way.

Stay focused, concentrate.

Narrator:

Kindness released the rock and hit a plate.

Love:

Amazing Kindness! Wonderful precision.

Creed:

Our boy has accuracy, we know what to give him.

Narrator:

Kindness didn't lose his focus.

He eyed the doe eating a crocus.

He pulled back on the bow's string,

And in the sun of gold, it gleamed.

The points of the arrow sparkled and twinkled.

His fingertips started to tingle.

He released one more calming sigh.

He shot his arrow in between the doe's eyes.

The doe fell over into the bed of blossoms.

He heard his mother shouting, *"Awesome!"*

He descended the tree,

With a smile and glee.

He pulled his arrow,

From the deceased doe.

Strength marched with his chest puffed.

He whistled and hummed and strutted his stuff.

He stopped at a tree that was different from the others.

It was surrounded by flowers, yellow in colour.

The bark was thicker, furrowed, and darker.

Strength examined the roots of the tree and its burrs.

He looked up at the leaves and in between,

The branches, chestnuts were dangling.

Strength grinned and cracked his thick knuckles.

He stood proud and flexed his muscles.

He wrapped his buff arms around the tree.

He shook it left and right easily.

The chestnuts rained down to the ground.

The yellow-green leaves flew all around.

Strength kept his stance; he didn't stumble or trip.

He rocked the tree without losing his grip.

His eyes were focused on the reddish nuts.

Strength laughed like a cretinous klutz.

His feet were grounded and did not move.

He was determined to have every nut removed

From the limbs of this tree that stood taller than he.

He bent his knees and rejoiced with glee.

The tree had become completely naked.

Free of nuts, leaves, and branches. Elated

Was Strength to see his fine work.

He pulled a bag from his purple skirt.

Strength gathered the nuts and placed them in his bag.

He couldn't wait to show his brothers and brag.

Then, by his face was a buzzing bee.

Strength:

Where there's bees, there's honey.

Narrator:

Brave found himself lost in the woods.

And as usual, he was no good.

He started to feel completely useless.

He looked around and became clueless.

He feared his brothers would berate him.

He knew they would continue to hate him.

He couldn't find a fruit, a nut, or a sprout.

He couldn't find a doe, a hare, or a trout.

He could hear Greed yelling, *"You are lousy and churlish!"*

He could hear Strength telling him, *"You're too dense."*

He could hear Kindness whispering, *"That doesn't make sense."*

His worries led him to run away.

He ran in panic as if he were prey

To a wolf, starving for three days.

He felt his blood pressure raise.

The voices of his brothers took over his brain.

His heart raced; his feet were strained.

His wolfy brothers expressed their anger.

He sweated and cried. He felt like an anchor

That weighed a ship down like he weighed down his family.

He felt Greed attack him manly and cannily.

Strength laughed at him thunderously.

Kindness questioned him wonderingly.

Brave pulled out his daggers and attacked his brothers.

They fought back and came at him from corners.

They fought and backed him into a stream.

He fell in the water and wanted to scream.

Then they were gone…his brother's voices were fading away.

He saw their shadows parading away.

His hands and daggers were under the water.

The beat of his heart was becoming shorter.

He felt peace, he felt relieved.

He smiled as if he felt nothing.

His mind was cleared.

The loathe disappeared.

He softly cheered.

Brave noticed the freshness of the water from the stream.

And from his bag, he pulled out four large canteens.

He filled the canteens up to the rim.

And happily, he hummed a hymn.

Strength carried his nuts while listening carefully,

To the buzzing song from the honeybees.

The buzz got louder as he continued to trot.

He stopped at a tree with a floral spot.

Dozens of bees were planted on lavender.

Strength:

I'm an excellent scavenger...

Or hunter.

Narrator:

Strength looked up at the tree to see a pendulous cylindrical hive.

He smiled at the beehive with a credulous egotistical drive.

He squatted down without taking his eyes off of the beehive.

He gained full focus on his target and began counting to five.

Strength:

One…

Narrator:

He counted. The sun

Warms his back and toasts his buns,

Browning him well-done.

Strength:

Two…

Narrator:

He counts. The wind blew,

Swinging the hive fro and to.

Up high, cockatoos

Fly 'round in the sky of blue,

Screeching at the strongest Few.

Strength:

Three…

Narrator:

He counted. The hollow pine tree,

Standing taller than he, and mighty,

Bent and curved and shed its leaves.

Strength:

Four…

Narrator:

He counted. His core

Muscles started to feel sore.

Sweat filled his face pores.

Strength:

Five!

Narrator:

He yelled and jumped high.

With both hands, he palmed the hive.

He fell on his back.

He heard some of his bones crack.

He felt no pain. He then laughed.

His fall alerted the entire woods.

It echoed and frightened his sweet goods.

He caused an earthquake that ran for miles.

The bees buzzed and gathered in piles.

All at once, they stung Strength,

Leaving his neck and hands in defect.

Strength:

Thank you, Kindness, for this helmet.

My face is safe and smooth like velvet.

I don't know what I'd do if my face were harmed.

I'd lose my strength and my charm.

Narrator:

He weakly rose up from the ground.

Like a child, he held the sweets he found.

In the woods, there was a cleared spot.

Greed waited for his brothers and sat on a log.

Strength approached him with swollen hands and neck.

Greed noticed and began to check.

Strength:

I was stung by bees.

Greed:

You'll be fine. You brought us sweets?

Strength:

And hazelnuts. What did you find, Greed?

Greed:

Grapes and berries.

Hopefully the other two found us meat.

Brave:

I'm here but… I only found water.

Strength:

If it isn't fresh, don't even bother.

Greed:

O, the water is fine.

I'll add the grapes and make us wine.

Where is Kindness?

Brave:

I couldn't guess.

Strength:

He better have gotten something good for us.

I am not just eating honey and hazelnuts.

Narrator:

Tired and completely worn out,

Kindness dragged his doe on the ground.

He had been pulling and pushing the doe for minutes.

He sweated and thirsted. He reached his limits.

His brothers heard him ruffling through the bushes.

Kindness grunted with each of his pushes.

He dragged the doe out of the woods. He fell to the ground exhausted.

His brothers saw the doe. They cheered and applauded.

Strength galloped over and gathered the doe.

Kindness crawled towards the group, weak and slow.

Strength:

Excellent job, Kindness! We're so proud.

Greed:

Now go back in the woods and search around.

We need sticks to make a fire and bring enough to make a basin.

When you come back, you'll help me build it.

Strength, I will get your medicine.

Brave, you section the venison.

And when you're healed, Strength, build us a tent.

Narrator:

The brothers did what they were ordered to do.

They used their tools to work and build.

The sun went down, the sky lost its blue.

The brothers showed they were uncommonly skilled.

The sky was black, and the crescent moon was bright.

Their faces were illuminated by the fire.

They finished their duties, ready to eat in the night.

The temperature dropped but the fire grew higher.

Greed:

Aye, which one of you can cook?

Strength:

Me, only with a book.

Brave:

I don't know how to cook anything.

What about you, Greed?

I thought you knew everything.

Greed:

I only know what needs to be known.

Name a king that has cooked for his own?

Brave:

The King of Cookery.

Greed:

Stop your foolery!

Strength:

But Greed, didn't you cook the swine?

Greed:

It was already cooked. All I did was put it in brine.

Kindness:

I cook, Greed.

Strength:

O, a hidden gift. Dost he?

Greed:

You're married, shouldn't your wife do the job?

Brave:

I've not seen dad cook for mom.

Kindness:

My wife and I are equals.

We do not follow prescribed roles.

Greed:

O, no wonder you're miserable.

Narrator:

Kindness sat at the table Strength had crafted.

He placed a curved pieced of wood on his lap and

Filled it with hazelnuts and crushed them.

His brothers watched and learned from him.

He covered all sides of the venison with nuts,

And next, the berries he started to crush.

The berries were juiced, and they started to gush.

The berries turned into a pureed slush.

He sat it aside and cooked the doe.

His brother watched this cooking show.

After browning the doe, he added the wine.

Fire blazed up into the sky.

The aroma of the wine was so devine.

His brothers were amazed to watch the fire fly.

They admired the fire as it turned pink.

They licked their lips, eager to eat!

Kindness set the doe aside to rest.

He cooked down the berries next.

The berries simmered and bubbled and popped.

Brave drooled as his mouth dropped.

The blues and reds made a melody.

They blended together in perfect harmony.

The aroma's got stronger but remained sweet.

Kindness cooked to its fragrant beat.

The wine had crescendoed the meal,

But the decrescendo was what they could feel.

He constructed the berries like an elite composer.

And when it was time, he approached his closer.

He added honey to thicken his sauce.

He held it high and began to toss.

He drizzled his sauce over the meat.

And just like a song, the meal was complete.

The brothers said grace and began their feast.

The delicious food made their moods increase.

The meat was cooked perfectly pink.

The juices stained their lips like ink.

Strength:

Kindness, you are truly gifted.

My spirit has been lifted!

Greed:

Save some for the rest of our mission.

Strength:

I can't help it, Greed. I'm a vigorous man.

Narrator:

They finished their first-class food,

Then slept in their tent under a quarter moon.

Scene **V**. Zaguah's Lair

Narrator:

The Few continued their journey.

They have walked and rested for days.

Greed followed the map and began to worry.

They were stuck in an endless maze.

They thirsted, they starved, they wanted to give up.

Their bodies were chafed and covered with bumps.

They swam through waters and climbed over mountains.

They missed the horses they once mounted.

They were stung by hornets and bitten by snakes.

They splashed their way through poisonous lakes.

Agony was shown across their faces.

They explored strange and chilling places.

They fell on their backs and scraped their knees.

Their blood was taken by mosquitos and fleas.

Greed had antidotes, but he was running low.

And although he searched, none could be shown.

Fungus grew on 'The Promising Few'.

Termites, too, ate their way through.

They found bamboo for them to chew.

But then the crew underwent the flu.

Their toes turned blue, their nose did, too.

They ran into a monstrous view.

They strapped their shoes as the wind blew.

They slept on dew that stuck like glue.

Every disaster Mother Nature threw,

'The Promising Few' fought their way through.

Kindness:

Where are we going next?

Strength:

Are we there yet?

Brave:

Can we please rest?

Greed:

You can shut thy mouths, or I'll remove thine necks!

We will get there when we get there,

And you will know we're there when we get there!

Kindness:

But where is there?

Greed:

Up thy posterior if thou care!

Ask another question! Thou dare?

Strength:

Settle down, Greed.

We're just…

Brave:

Hungry!

Greed:

You two ate the entire doe!

You ate it all three days ago!

There's nothing here, nothing around.

Just an empty plain and this blackened ground.

Narrator:

Greed was right, there was nothing in sight.

The ground was black, the clouds were grey.

There were no trees, there was no light.

They couldn't tell if it was night or day.

They continued to argue, they continued to complain.

They continued their journey in disarray.

While he ignored his argumentative brothers,

Kindness noted the temperatures.

Kindness:

My hair is curling and getting frizzy.

Strength:

And what does that mean?

Kindness:

That means that the humidity is rising.

It's hot, very hot. I'm sweating.

Brave:

A sudden change in weather. I feel it.

Greed:

A sudden change in location. We made it.

Narrator:

The brothers walked around a tall boulder.

The boulder and rocks were dark blue in colour.

The ground was too, but it was also cracked.

And inside the cracks, lava was packed.

The volcanic lava bursted from open holes in the ground.

The brothers walked up to a blue cave they found.

Although it was black from the entrance,

They could see the lava blinking from within it.

Strength:

This- this is it? The Sucrex Cave?

Greed:

No, we'll be there in about four days.

Kindness:

But where are we?

Narrator:

And just before Greed could speak.

A dragon's head broke through the top of the cave.

This dragon was purple; its skin was waved.

It had fiery orange hair lined down its back.

Its wings blew heat around as they flapped.

The dragon's eyes were an emerald green.

Sharp and yellow were its teeth.

It had black claws longer than its hair.

The dragon screeched and blew fire in the air.

As the dragon settled back down in its lair.

The scared brothers cried and said a prayer.

Strength:

A dragon's lair?! You knew we were coming to a dragon's lair?!

Greed:

Yes, but I didn't know the dragon was alive! I swear!

Strength:

O, you didn't know? You didn't know the dragon was alive? You fooled us!

Greed:

I remember the stories our parents told us.

They said they defeated Zaguah!

Kindness:

Maybe it's an offspring.

Strength:

Zaguah had a baby!?

Greed:

Zaguah's a male, he can't have a baby!

Kindness:

I said maybe.

Maybe he had a lady.

Strength:

Well, who's going to defeat this dragon, Greed?

Kindness:

He, Greed.

Greed:

Me!? Not me!

Why not Strength, "The Almighty"?

Strength:

I'm not skilled at mythical beings.

And besides, this is Brave's dream.

Brave:

What? Me?

This isn't my dream!

Strength:

Of course, it is, according to He.

Brave:

Who is He?

Strength:

The one narrating this story.

Narrator:

It is true Brave; it is your dream.

Shall I remind thee?

"O, how I hate to introduce this part.

The third brother, and eternal brain fart,

Is Brave. He is one team player.

He hopes to become a dragon slayer."

Brave:

But, why me?

I don't want this dream!

Narrator:

Because it is written by She.

Strength:

And who is She?

Narrator:

The creator of thee.

The creator of Creed.

The creator of Love, the creator of me.

Kindness:

The one who wrote this mystery.

Greed:

It is an adventure, actually.

Enhanced with a bit of poetry.

Brave:

Who cares about the poetic She!?

Defeating this dragon is not my dream!

Greed:

What is it, Brave? What are you trying to say?

Strength:

Are you saying that you're not brave?

Greed:

Brave not brave?

An ironic shame.

Kindness:

What do you say? Are you not brave, Brave?

Brave:

No! Or yes. I'm saying that I'm scared.

I am not prepared!

Greed:

Being scared means you are not brave.

Brave:

No, I'm Brave!

Strength:

But you're not of brave.

Greed:

Of bravery.

Strength:

There is no need for you to correct me!

Kindness:

Can we just figure this out please?

Greed:

Of course, we just need Brave to be who he is!

Brave:

But why not Strength?

Strength:

Because it is written.

Brave:

What's written of me should not be writ!

Kindness:

That doesn't make sense.

Brave:

You doesn't make sense!

Greed:

Brave! Strength! One of you go in and defeat that damn dragon!

Strength:

But why us? You're the eldest!

Brave:

You're supposed to protect us!

Greed:

Stop this nonsense! You are Brave.

Brave:

Am I Brave?

Strength:

Could you be brave?

Brave:

Could I?

Strength:

Could you!?

Brave:

Should I?

Strength:

Would you!?

Kindness:

Stop! Stop! Stop! Stop! Stop! Stop this.

Narrator:

The brothers silenced.

Kindness:

We can defeat this lap…

The same way we did the others.

Greed:

And how is that?

Kindness:

Together.

But we need a plan…

We need a plan…

Greed?

Greed:

I'm thinking!

…I'm thinking.

Narrator:

They stood outside Zaguah's Lair silently waiting.

Greed looked around at the scorching land thinking and pacing.

He looked up at the green sky and saw a full moon inching forward.

He walked up to the entrance of the cave and drew his shield and sword.

Greed:

Follow me.

Narrator:

Said Greed.

They followed him into the lair to see the dragon strangely waiting.

It smiled down at the brothers, loudly growling and huffing and puffing.

In the blazing magma on a floating rock, the dragon was perched.

The dragon eyed its prey, hoping they would mistakenly lurch.

There were two stairways, one left and one right, lined up against the walls.

The dragon guarded an exit behind it, but they noticed several halls.

The brothers stood side by side. Strength stood tall, Brave with daggers in hands.

Kindness placed an arrow on his bow, and they waited for Greed's plan.

As smart and daring as he was, Greed

Had nothing in his mind to supply.

Strength:

What is the plan, Greed?

Greed:

The plan…do not die.

Narrator:

Greed charged towards the towering dragon and leaped over the bubbling matter.

He stabbed its foot as he landed, and his younger brothers began to scatter.

As the dragon screeched in pain, Kindness ascended the stairs on the left.

The dragon dropped his head back and Kindness aimed for its neck.

Kindness released several arrows, but they didn't do any good.

Greed struggled to remove his sword from the dragon's thick foot.

Strength approached the dragon; he removed the sword and passed it to Greed.

He grabbed the dragon's lengthy tail, he gripped it tight and attempted to swing

The dragon. He pulled and pulled, but it seemed useless.

The mightiest Few was weak and clueless.

Just when he decided to almost give up,

He lifted the dragon and screamed through his lungs.

The pain he felt from lifting this monster

Destroyed his body and perfect posture.

As he leaned to swing this enormous beast,

His hair fell into the lava, but Greed

Grabbed his purple vested chest

And pulled him up, with his best.

Strength's helmet fell into the lava, it sank and slowly melted.

The dragon fell into the rocky wall, and it angrily belted.

The lair shook from the dragon's fall, knocking Kindness off the steps.

Kindness dangled from the top of the steps, but he pulled himself over the cliff.

Brave stood from down below watching his brothers lose the war.

He was wondering and realised it was he, the weakest amongst the four,

Who had to defeat the dragon. So, he ran fearlessly up the right steps.

He reached the top and pulled out his daggers, he jumped onto the dragon's neck.

He shoved his daggers into its neck and slid down leaving an open slit.

The dragon fell and broke the ground. Strength wrapped his arms around its neck firmly.

Kindness aimed an arrow at its eye and positioned himself on his knee sternly.

He waited patiently and took deep breaths before releasing his arrow string.

The point of the arrow shined and shimmered as he eyed his target carefully.

Finally, he released the arrow, and it flew at a remarkable speed.

It struck the dragon in its left eye, causing it to bleed.

The dragon cried and mourned, but it only became more annoyed.

It blindly swiped its large arm, throwing Brave across the lair.

Brave fell unconscious. He couldn't move, for his body was destroyed.

He spat, choked, and coughed up blood. The dragon polluted the air.

The dragon's burning blazing breath

Left Brave battered, black, and blue.

Brave, broken and browned to death,

Was boggled. He bled his body through.

Kindness cried, and cramped, and crumbled as he shot his arrows towards the dragon.

He couldn't control his shaking hands as he was breathing in the rock fragments.

Kindness crawled crookedly around the gruesome cobbed cave.

Composure, cures, and contentment were things he currently craved.

Strength staggered, struggled, and stammered as he punched the beast continuously.

He sobbed, snotted, stirred, and suffered as he strangled the dragon strenuously.

The strong saviour strained his body as he struck this savage being.

He stormed around and sweated heavily. His sweat stopped him from seeing.

Greed grabbed his sword. He grunted and growled vigorously at the grotesque beast.

Greed grieved as its green blood covered his body so greatly.

Greed gathered himself, though he wasn't strong, he gave his best and gave his all.

Greed groaned and moaned, and griped and gasped, as he watched his brothers fall.

Greed looked over across the lava to see Brave unconscious on the ground.

He saw Brave's daggers next to him. What was glistening white and round,

Were the pearls. They were blinking at Greed, as if they were giving him a clue.

Greed looked up at the top of the lair where the dragon had broken through.

And inching to the centre of the hole, was the brightest and fullest moon.

Greed:

Brave! Brave!

Wake up, Brave!

Narrator:

Brave slowly turned his head towards Greed

Who was in anguish, yelling towards he.

Greed:

Brave! Brave! You must use your daggers, Brave!

The moon is centred above the cave!

Use the pearls, Brave!

Brave:

I…I ca– I can't…

Greed:

Yes! Yes, you can!

Only you can do it, Brave. This battle is meant for you!

"The pearls: as round and white as thee,

Rare and always glistening.

Hold it up to the moon,

And it will tell you what to do…"

Get up, Brave! You must use the pearls. It's you!

Grab your daggers and hold them to the moon!

Brave:

Why…?

I…

Greed:

It's you! It's always been you! It is written!

This is your mission!

Narrator:

Brave reached over and palmed his daggers. He saw the pearls glistening bright.

He struggled to stand upright as he examined the pearls in white.

He saw his brothers fighting the dragon, he saw them dying and heard them cry.

He looked up to see half of the moon resting in the sky.

He stumbled and staggered slowly up the stairs on the right.

He sat at the top of the steps, waiting for the moon to position right.

His brothers continued their restless fight.

Watching them lose was a dreadful sight.

At last, the moon was centred.

Brave held up his golden daggers.

He lined the pearls up against each other.

He formed an 'x' and felt a shudder.

The pearls beamed brightly,

So bright, they were blinding.

The pearls lit up the entire lair.

They blew a sparkling wind through his hair.

Brave squinted his eyes to look in the stone.

His eyes widened after seeing what was shown.

He put down his daggers and turned towards the dragon.

He looked down at his brothers and ended their agon.

Brave:

ZAGUAH!!

Narrator:

He screamed. The dragon flew up.

His brothers silenced and hid as Brave and the dragon looked eye to eye.

The dragon frowned and grunted at Brave's angry voice, but still, it complied.

Brave:

I am Brave of Hazelton.

I am one fourth of The Promising Few.

My brothers and I are on a mission,

And you refuse to let us through.

We mean no harm for you and your home.

We only wish to return to our own.

We are more than great; we exceed the vast

Of men. And I am more than a mindless heat of breath.

If you continue refuse to let me and my brother's past,

The only option left for you is death.

A death that will be marked in history.

A death that will be MY victory!

Narrator:

The dragon grinned at Brave's daring speech.

It blew a ring of fire and brutally screeched.

The dragon and Brave were both ready to fight.

His brother's watched as Brave took flight.

He jumped and placed both daggers into

The dragon's chest as the dragon flew.

The dragon closed its wings and held Brave tight.

They fell to the ground and the daggers gave light.

A light so bright, it nearly blinded his brothers.

The daggers gave light in many a-colours.

They listened to Brave's desperate scream.

His voice was loud, deep, and extreme.

Though they could not see him through the colourful beam.

They knew that Brave would save the team.

The colours soon dimmed and Brave's voice died.

His brothers ran towards him and stood side by side.

Brave was still wrapped in the dragon's wings,

And from down beneath, his feet were hanging.

Strength pulled the dragon's heavy wings apart.

And there was Brave with his daggers in its heart.

Its chest was cut open, blood was flowin'.

And with no emotion, Brave had spoken.

Brave:

Can I…can I keep it?

Greed:

Keep what, kid?

Brave:

The heart.

Greed:

No, you cannot keep the heart!

Get up, get out of this!

Help me clean him, Kindness.

Narrator:

Kindness and Greed dried Brave of blood.

They drained his boots and wrung his gloves.

Strength removed the daggers from the dragon's heart.

He held them up to the moon and looked into the gems.

Nothing happened. He saw nothing but stars.

He cleaned the blood and placed them in Brave's hands.

Strength:

I don't know how you did it, but I am impressed.

Brave:

The stones only work for me, I guess.

Kindness:

Tell us, Brave, what did you see?

Brave:

I saw me.

Before entering this cave,

I was afraid.

But I saw myself, I saw Brave.

And after myself, I saw a heart.

I saw my daggers in the dragon's heart.

I know I am not smart. But the daggers made me feel I had a part.

They helped me be brave, they helped me be smart.

I do not know how to explain it, but…it's hard.

Greed:

Such powerful objects should not be held by you.

You didn't even know what you could do.

Strength:

Brave, you were very potent.

Even I was afraid, I admit.

You did something I could not do.

I am very proud of you.

Greed:

O Strength, I wish we could say the same about you.

Come on! Let's move.

Narrator:

As the brothers exited the lair they began choking on smog.

They were surrounded by a thick black fog.

They coughed and choked, but they made it through.

They ached in pain, so they took a few

Moments to rest

And catch their breaths.

Kindness:

That was one hell of a duel.

Brave:

O, Kindness! Did you see me? Did you see what I do?

My beautiful daggers! The pearls, the jewels!

My babies, I don't know what I'd do without you.

Greed:

You mean me.

You don't know what you'd do without me!

Strength:

We all fought that dragon, equally.

We are a team.

Greed:

Ha! Kindness was great.

Amazing was Brave.

But you Strength, you're no God,

But a fraud.

Strength:

I'm not sure I'm following thee.

Greed:

O, stop the stupidity!

You couldn't save us from that damned bear!

The Swallowing Swamp, that dragon there,

I had to tell you all what to do to get us here, safe!

'The Mighty Strength', a fake!

Kindness:

Greed, we all had a part in each of those obstacles.

Greed:

O, shut up, imbecile!

My brain is the only reason why we're alive and you know it!

He claims to be the best of all, but he sure doesn't show it.

Narrator:

Greed took his handkerchief and cleaned his sword.

He kept the dragon's blood as an award.

Strength watched him with a frown upon his face.

He spoke deeply and mighty and began to pace.

Strength:

Smartness.

Narrator:

Greed grabbed his robe for him to dress.

He, confusingly, looked Strength's way.

Greed:

What did you say?

Strength:

Smartness.

Greed:

What is this?

Strength:

Your name is Smartness.

Greed:

No, it isn't. Ask the kids.

Strength:

They may not know because they're much younger.

But I know you, older brother.

I was born one year later,

And I do, vaguely, remember…

That your name is Smartness.

Brave:

I don't understand a tad.

Have you gone mad?

Strength:

HIS NAME IS SMARTNESS!

And he's changed it.

And we must know why, we insist.

Narrator:

Greed dressed himself with his red robe.

He looked at the sky of red and purple.

He placed his sword into his sheath.

He felt his blood boiling from beneath.

He strapped his sword onto his firm back,

He turned to Strength and looked down at the cracks

On the rocks he was standing on with aggression.

He looked high up at Strength to answer his question.

Greed:

With Smartness, we need everything.

But with Greed, what do we need?

No one wants a man of greed to handle their money.

But with Smartness, they gain trust.

"We'll hand him our money to count it up."

I'll add them up and multiply.

And when it's time,

I'll subtract and divide.

And what do they find?

A missing dime.

So, they change their mind

With having me find.

That is why I

Choose to be defined

As Greed rather than Smartness,

Because Greed gets some rest.

Brave:

You're…crazy.

Strength:

He's lazy!

Kindness:

Love and Creed

Made us, Greed,

To help the people in need.

But you'd rather sleep?

Strength:

What you just said was very unlawful.

You'd rather spend the time away

Doing what makes you joyful,

Knowing that people's lives are at stake?

You have the strongest gift amongst us four,

And yet you'd rather be a bore.

To be alone in peace and quiet

With no duty or service.

Would those things you rather do?

Greed:

Wouldn't you?

You hear those people's cries.

You should be tired the most.

But every morning you rise,

You comb your hair, and you boast.

And what do you get in return? Broken bones.

Kindness knows.

Strength:

Well, if you don't want to take on such responsibilities,

Why are you fighting to become a king?

Greed:

Because I am Greed.

Narrator:

Greed smiled and chuckled, then turned away.

He walked cockily and led the way.

They walked only for a couple of minutes.

They stopped at an empty lot for a good night's rest.

The moon was full, but the sky was red.

On the cold hard ground, they made their bed.

Greed made sure Brave and Strength were asleep.

He turned over to Kindness and began to speak.

Greed:

Kindness.

Kindness:

Yes.

Narrator:

Kindness saw a worried look in Greed's eyes.

They both sat up and began whispering.

Greed:

I couldn't sleep. I've been staring at the skies.

Kindness:

Is there something you need from me?

Narrator:

Before speaking, Greed looked off into the distance.

He was thinking. He then looked back at Kindness.

Greed:

Sometimes my smartness is a poison.

I know things I wish I didn't.

It's stressful being the one everyone turns to when they need advice, but it's even more stressful when I've none.

And sometimes I do have the answer they're looking for but lying is what's best for them.

And though it is my will,

The truth can hurt but being the messenger could kill.

Kindness:

Greed, I've never heard you speak like this.

Or to me, that is.

Why do you say these things now? Why the telling lips?

Greed:

Because you are Kindness.

You're probably the best.

You do not complain, you do not fuss. You—

You always listen. And I thought maybe…I thought maybe I can trust you.

Narrator:

Kindness would never spill a secret. Kindness would never kiss and tell.

He made it easy for Greed to speak up, easy for him to dwell.

He and Greed were never close, they were never cordial males.

Kindness never thought his oldest brother would look to him for help.

With Greed being the oldest and Kindness being the youngest, they never spent a day together.

But that night, Kindness felt his older brother.

Act III

Scene I. Sucrex City

Narrator:

A few days later, the brothers reached a site.

Bones, ashy homes, and pale grass were in their sight.

The ground, the buildings, and the sky was white.

The dead city felt dark, though its colour was light.

Skulls were scattered around and about.

Windows were shattered on an empty house.

Not a single person was found throughout

The city. No birds, no plants, not even a mouse.

Strength:

What in the Heavens happened here? Where is the life? Where are the people?

Greed:

Nevar and Willa. Their powers are evil.

This is a city they once controlled.

The Pope was right, they've destroyed many cities.

I wonder how powerful are these two beings.

Brave:

The Willa said she helped the Pope and Love and Creed.

Kindness:

But the Pope said they've falsified stories.

Strength:

They did indeed.

Or did they, Greed?

Did our parents make you and me?

Or did the witches make Love and Creed.

Greed:

I'm unsure I know the answer to that.

But it's true, the witches helped mom and dad.

Kindness:

But something seems off, this doesn't seem right.

Are Willa and Nevar good or not?

They've helped our parents with their life.

But they've also destroyed cities. They have powers like God?

Are their powers so strong?

Greed:

Nothing in life comes free.

There is always a price to pay.

They gave great things to Love and Creed.

But there were some things they took away.

Narrator:

The brothers walked through the silent city.

They examined what once used to be living.

Brave:

I cannot wait to meet Nevar, that being.

Her story must be interesting.

For her to destroy an entire city,

She must be better than Love and Creed.

Strength:

Nothing exceeds Love and Creed.

Kindness:

But God?

Strength:

Not even He.

Kindness:

Dad wrote about God for a cause.

Greed:

But did he even obey the heavenly laws?

Being born first, I saw our parents live.

I saw their mistakes and heard their give.

You were right, Kindness, about The Commandments.

They weren't placed to protect any of us,

They were placed to control Hazelton.

Father wanted nothing but authority.

And when Mailo wouldn't allow him,

He and mom would flee.

When they left, they made Hazelton in hopes that they'd be worshipped.

And successfully, they were, and as a gift to the people, they birthed us.

Kindness:

How do you know this?

This can't be the truth!

Greed:

Don't be naive, Kindness.

Look at me, look at you.

How do you think we got our gifts?

No one is born with such talent.

Gifts like these were crafted,

Made special by a witch.

And if you honestly do not believe the things I say.

Ask Nevar when we reach her cave.

Strength:

None of this makes any sense to me.

Brave:

I agree.

Strength:

If our father wrote of religion but didn't practise,

Why did he make us and Hazelton do so? Why did he write it?

Greed:

Behind every religious aspect, Creed is.

If he could persuade a mass of people to believe in religion,

He could persuade them to believe in him.

He hid himself inside of religious scrolls,

And God he'll be, he hoped so.

But unfortunately, death took a toll.

Brave:

O, their tragic death! Hey, isn't it strange how mom and dad died together in the Hall?

Greed:

No, it isn't strange at all.

Kindness:

Y'know, Brave, I think you're onto something.

They died of suicide, that I don't believe.

As Greed said, dad wanted to be worshipped.

He wouldn't have killed himself with that powerful mindset.

Maybe someone broke into the temple and assassinated them.

Maybe it was someone jealous and smarter than them.

Maybe someone wanted something they had, and when they denied him,

He killed them.

Maybe mom tried to stop him, but her love could not stop him.

Maybe that same someone, stole from them and wanted something they were to give,

But not to give to him.

Maybe…

Greed:

Maybe you have something to say, Kindness.

What is this?

Hmmm? Maybe there's something you're hiding, yes?

Speak your mind, there's something you know?

Something you want to show?

No?

I thought so.

Narrator:

Kindness looked down and slightly whimpered.

When Greed walked away, Kindness then whispered.

Kindness:

It's my wife, she's sick.

Cancer, or- I don't know what it is.

She's very ill and I left her…alone, to raise our kids.

I left to come on this trip.

I'm-I'm a terrible husband, I guess.

She's been sick for quite some time.

Every night, she would lie down and whine.

She can barely walk,

I can't remember the last time she talked.

Brave:

No!

Strength:

My...Kindness, I'm so sorry.

Greed:

How come you've not said a thing,

A thing to me!?

Kindness:

Because I'm afraid of you, Greed.

You're not very pleasant to me.

And plus, we've all been busy.

The citizens of Hazelton have been in much need.

Strength:

Screw the people of Hazelton! Fat-kidneyed they are!

You come first; you are our brother!

Greed:

Kindness, what does she look like?

Kindness:

Pale, very white.

Bags under both her eyes.

She is losing hair, and there's lumps on her chest.

Her lips are black, and she can barely catch her breath.

Greed:

It sounds like a fever,

But the lumps could be cancer.

Kindness, when we return home, I will make a cure.

I have medicine and herbs that you must give to her.

Kindness:

Well, that sounds promising.

Thank you, Greed.

Greed:

Whatever you need.

Narrator:

Greed hugged Kindness for the first time in their lives.

It was long and warm. They both had watery eyes.

It was the first time Kindness had been close or even embraced his eldest brother.

He cherished every second of it and enjoyed Greed's scent of clover.

A few steps ahead, there was a high mountain.

They looked up at it, but the top was clouded.

Greed pulled out the map and then he noted.

Greed:

The Sucrex Cave is at the top of this mountain.

Scene II. Mount Paramountain

Brave:

Just how are we going to climb this?

You think my daggers will assist?

Greed:

There is no moon in sight, genius.

Strength:

Just like the swamp, I could toss you all up.

Greed:

What!?

Strength:

Or get on my back and I will jump.

Greed:

I don't want broken bones or crushed lungs.

I'm all out of medicines.

The only way up is to climb it.

Kindness:

I have this.

Narrator:

Kindness pulled out his grappling hook.

His brothers gave him a confused look.

Greed:

What is this?

Narrator:

Greed asked while snatching it.

Kindness:

It's a grappling hook. I figured we needed it.

It's new, something you haven't invented.

Greed:

I've invented this.

Just a bit…different.

And where did you get this?

Kindness:

At the City of Hahm, I…I stole it.

Strength:

Whoa-ho-ho!

Brave:

Kindness stole!?

Greed:

You sneaky, slimy rascal!

I knew you had it in ya!

Come here! I love ya!

Narrator:

Greed kissed Kindness on his left cheek.

Kindness:

I only stole it because you wouldn't give me money.

Greed:

Well, now you can have whatever you need.

Money, knowledge, a cure for your honey.

When we go back home, it's just you and me!

Okay Strength, do the thing.

Strength:

What thing?

Greed:

The swinging thing.

Strength:

O, I see.

Narrator:

Strength grabbed the hook and swung it 'round and around.

His arm moved so quickly in speed.

He tossed the hook high, and it landed on grounds.

He tugged on the rope,

Strength:

Yep. It's sturdy.

Greed:

Brave, cut off your sleeves with your daggers.

Brave:

I am Brave the Dragon Slayer.

Greed:

Brave the Dragon Slayer,

Will you cut off your sleeves with your daggers?

Brave:

Sure, but why?

Greed:

To make gloves for us so we can climb.

Brave:

But I already have gloves.

Greed:

Not for you, US!

Narrator:

Greed used Braves sleeves to craft them gloves.

He grabbed the rope and pulled himself up.

His younger brothers followed right after,

Ready to take on the next disaster.

Their hands were sore, and their muscles weakened.

It felt like years though it was only seconds,

As the brothers climbed closer to the cliff.

They stopped five feet from the entrance of the Sucrex Cave.

They stood and shivered from the cool wind it gave.

Scene III. The Sucrex Cave

Narrator:

They entered the cold dark cave. Orange candles were lit but slightly dimmed.

They saw tables and potions neatly placed. They saw a bubbling cauldron, thick rimmed.

A curved staircase led to a dark corner. They heard a charming voice and drew their weapons.

They looked up the staircase to see a figure of the strange woman that had suddenly spoken.

Nevar:

Look at you, "The Promising Few",

Promising things that won't come true,

Running around like whining babies,

Acting weak though gifted greatly!

Though, it was fun watching your journey,

Watching you work harder than what you should have.

I watched you scream, fall, run, and worry.

I've watched you win and fail, and cry and laugh.

The gifts I bestowed upon you few,

Wasted! Gone before it ever grew!

My wonderful work, given to a group of substandard men

More worried about overcoming impotence.

I should have known by the appearance of Creed,

That he and Love would give birth to such common beings!

Now look at you fools standing before me!

Only here to forever bore me!

Strength:

How dare you flip your tongue at us!?

You speak mighty yet bogus!

Brave:

We are not some whiny children.

Greed:

We are the 'Promising Few of Hazelton'!

Kindness:

We've worked hard to build our names.

We help the poor and protect the lame.

Strength:

We have high profiles!

Greed:

Notable reputations!

Kindness:

We need not a witch, a God.

Brave:

Nor even a vacation!

Greed:

We have smarts!

Strength:

Strength!

Kindness:

Hearts!

Brave:

And bravery!

Nevar:

Yet you stand before me in desperate need.

Narrator:

The brothers stood silently in defeat.

Nevar walked up into the golden light.

The brothers stood tall without a fright.

She wore a beautiful, well fitted, orange cloak.

Her skin was as brown as bark from an oak.

She glided gently on her feet.

She descended the stairs and began to speak.

Nevar:

You've travelled far and high

Just to reach my site.

You walked miles and miles,

Battled the toughest battles.

You have the smarts to be a king, but frugal are your pockets.

And you, sir, have the power but they need more than your strength.

Kind yet naïve, dumb but brave.

Some of these advantages came into play,

But you let your low qualities stand in the way.

And that is what brings you here today.

Brave:

Actually, we're here to become king.

Nevar:

...I see.

But now let's see if those low qualities

Will be a problem after this meeting.

You are all here because you each

Seek to become king, and I can help indeed.

But it won't be easy.

Narrator:

Nevar stood at a podium a few feet away from the brothers.

The look on their faces was frail and bothered.

Nevar:

So, let's talk about who will be king.

And I will give you all time to think.

In my cauldron,

Is a boiling potion.

And with a spell, one of you will be chosen.

This spell will make one of you king,

And you will hold the title immediately.

No other man will be named king,

After the chosen one takes a drink.

This potion and spell are everlasting.

It will be marked down in history.

It cannot, shall not, and will not be undone.

There is nothing I can do once the spell is done.

You will feel no side effects to this potion.

You will feel nothing but happiness once the spell is in motion.

You will return home, you will reign.

You will feel powerful. The others will feel pain.

Greed:

What's the catch?

Nevar:

Excuse me?

Greed:

Your contract is missing a patch.

What do we sacrifice to become king?

Nevar:

The spell will bring some difficulties.

I see red and brown for the chosen king.

I see heat and greys for him and his city.

I see misunderstandings.

I see fires of clay

Coming his way.

But I also see salvation.

I see a wise reparation.

Will it be you, Greed? Or will it be Strength.

A man tall and mighty, well-fit for the position.

But Greed, your city needs your smartness.

When I look at you, I see a largeness,

A largeness of royalty and money.

It's like you're born to be king.

But again, we have Strength.

Very, very dominant.

Even Sir Salas must admit.

You as king would make Hazelton dynamic!

Brave:

But what about me?

I deserve to be king!

Do you see it?

The skills, the passion, I have it!

Nevar:

Yes! I see it. After all, you are the one who slayed the dragon.

Kindness:

Maybe this is all a trick…

Nevar:

Kindness, this is no time to be hesitant.

You are the one they voted for.

You are the one best for the chore.

Tell me, who is it that wants to be king?

Greed, tell me, do you agree?

Narrator:

Greed glanced at Brave's waist where his daggers rested.

The rubies were blinking, their light reflected.

Greed had thought hard, Greed thought long.

He gave her an answer, hoping it wasn't wrong.

Greed:

After listening to your terms and conditions,

And peeping through the fine print,

I realise who I really am,

And that I do not need Hazelton.

There's something strange going on here,

And something terrible is going to occur.

I'll just take my robe here,

And return to where we were.

I'm not saying I don't want to be king,

And no, I have not lost an ounce of greed.

But that potion there, bubbling in green,

Is made for someone dumb or naïve.

As much as I would like to accept this,

I put my place in as secessus.

Strength:

Sick, sec, what?

Brave:

Six sexes.

Kindness:

Successes.

Greed:

Secessus.

In other words, from Lord Charles L.,

"I withdraw, rebel."

Nevar:

You have proved the smartest greed.

Or maybe you've proved the dumbest generosity.

Remove yourself from my cave,

And let me consult with Brave.

Narrator:

Greed slowly exited the circle and walked towards the entrance of the cave. He looked back at Strength, and they locked eyes.

Strength was confused as to why someone like Greed would back away. He then remembered Greed has always been wise.

Nevar filled a flask with the green potion,

Carefully from her black cauldron.

Brave:

I see nothing wrong with this. Green is my favourite flavour.

Nevar:

So, will you do the favour?

Strength:

Witch!

My whole life I have been called narcissistic.

Some say it's a curse, I say it's a gift.

But I'm not feeling so confident

About this contract or this trip.

I might've missed something important here,

Or overlooked what you prepared.

But my brother, Greed, was born smart and,

I believe he caught on to your bargain.

And knowing his intelligence, and knowing his heart,

I shall take those things in regard.

That is why I shall follow in his steps.

But that does not mean I have lost my strength.

So, I say unto you, ominous witch,

I decline the throne of Hazelton.

Nevar:

Really, Strength? Is it not your name?

Maybe you aren't as strong as you claim.

Hmm, I would have never guessed it.

But it's alright. You may now exit.

Narrator:

Strength exited the cave but was then stopped

Outside by Greed, who was toying with rocks.

Greed:

Hello, good brother. Shall we go?

Strength:

We shall. But first, I must know,

It seemed your love for becoming king

Was ever so strong and guaranteed.

So, then I wonder why you, Greed,

Were the first to back down and the first to leave?

Narrator:

Greed and Strength stopped in their tracks. Strength waited patiently for a response.

They walked closer to the edge of the mountain. Greed sighed and explained his thoughts.

Greed:

Out of the four of us, it is me,

Born sharp-witted, born with greed.

And, sometimes, I think I overthink.

But something's shifty with being king,

Well, being the King of Hazelton.

And I know one thing about that potion.

Strength:

What is it brother? What do you know?

Greed:

Something horrible and I shall not show.

And you may not possess the brains of me,

But even you, a man of conceit,

Felt a bit odd about this meet'.

That is why you left and you're here with me.

We four brothers are blessed with great,

So many skills on our plates.

But the throne has torn us four apart,

And shown what really lies within our hearts.

We're destined for greatness, proficient for sure.

No other man can compare to us four!

But that potion is too strong, for three at least.

But even you, Strength, have become weak.

And I, a man of greed,

Backed away from royalty.

Have I gone dumb, or am I too smart?

Do you see, Strength, why we part

Away from that deal the witch presented?

Did I overthink this one mission?

Or am I weary of opulence?

And have you realised your humbleness?

Something strange is happening to us,

And I'm a bit worried for Brave and Kindness.

Strength:

But where will we go now, older brother?

Greed:

You go back to Hazelton; I'll go to another.

Strength:

And what will you do?

Greed:

I'll do what I do!

I'll take my money and I'll fix this hitch.

And besides, I listened closely to that witch,

And what the hag said was quite interesting.

We have desires; she has a prophecy.

And I have a plan on becoming king.

Narrator:

Greed descended the mountain, but Strength stayed.

He wanted to wait on Kindness and Brave.

Nevar continued pressuring Brave and Kindness.

She proved which ones of The Few were spineless.

Nevar:

Brave, you were Brave enough to slay the dragon.

Will you be Brave enough to take this potion?

Brave:

Well, of course. I don't see why not.

I don't see anything wrong with this bubbling pot.

Kindness:

Brave! Stop! Do not drink it.

We need to talk, to think about this.

I think it's dangerous.

Brave:

Why do you say that, Kindness?

Kindness:

Because Greed and Strength,

They left.

Brave, I...I don't know what to tell you.

You deserve to be king, but not this way.

You…I- I don't know what to do.

Let's go home! Let's turn away.

Brave:

No way!

We've come this far.

And we can't turn down the beautiful Nevar.

Kindness:

Brave…I cannot lose you.

I cannot choose, too.

I don't know what to do.

I know the truth,

But I don't know what to do.

Narrator:

Kindness pulled Brave near.

He whispered in his ear:

Kindness:

Do not choose.

Brave:

But I cannot lose.

What about you?

Kindness:

I cannot choose…

But my people need me.

Look at their poverty!

They need someone to set them free.

Nevar:

Yes, I agree.

But shall it be

A man with kindness or stupidity?

Kindness:

But o, the pain this potion shall bring!

Should I save myself, or this city?

What will the people come to think

Of a man of kindness who's selfish and weak?

Nevar:

How interesting, the kindness in he.

Maybe he isn't so naïve.

Do you back down? Will you bend the knee?

Or will you be the chosen king?

Kindness:

But I cannot be king, it's not written.

I have a wife, and I have kids.

I need more time to ponder your give.

I admit, I'm afraid of the future I'll live.

Brave:

But me, I'm not afraid of anything!

Hand me this tube of absolute doom!

And let me do what I'm destined to!

Kindness:

Brave! Wait!

Narrator:

But it was too late!

Brave had drunk the potion from the flask.

He swallowed, burped, and stretched his back.

Nevar:

The potion will not work without the spell.

Brave:

O, well…

Narrator:

Brave turned to Kindness who was teary eyed.

Kindness:

Do whatever brings you pride.

Narrator:

Brave smiled and turned back to the witch.

Brave:

I am ready to strike it rich!

Narrator:

Nevar refilled the flask with the potion.

She walked up to Brave, and the flask glistened.

She quoted the spell and Kindness listened.

Nevar:

With the powers of Oogabaloo,

With the waters of The Black Lagoon,

Make this man of bravery King,

And bring him everlasting royalty.

From the mountains of high and the oceans of low,

I bestow this crown that no other can hold.

No man or woman, nor child or infant,

Shall ever be named ruler of Hazelton.

Not now or later, nor after his demise.

No one can ever touch this noble prize!

And unto this man, forever he reigns,

And carries the duties, along with the pains.

Though adversity may come in response to this spell,

It cannot be undone, nor can He repel.

This man of bravery concurs this makutu,

And drinks this potion with ample gratitude.

Narrator:

Nevar poured the sparkling potion into Brave's mouth.

He burped and released a green cloud.

Nevar:

I present to you, "King Brave of Hazelton".

Brave:

And Dragon Slayer. Say it!

Nevar:

I present to you, "King Brave of Hazelton, the Dragon Slayer".

Brave:

Yes! It is me! I am greater!

Kindness:

How do you feel?

Brave:

I feel…real!

I'm fine Kindness, see?

No need to worry.

Kindness:

Nevar, the side effects. Are you sure there are none?

Narrator:

They turned around, but Nevar was gone.

Scene IV. Mount Paramount

Narrator:

Kindness exited the cave and met up with Strength.

Strength stood tall and stared blankly at Kindness.

Kindness stalely smiled and felt nervous.

Brave ran out of the cave feeling joyous.

Brave:

HAHAH! Bow down to me peasant!

I am your King of Hazelton!

Kindness:

And Dragon Slayer. Say it!

Narrator:

Kindness joked and smiled.

Strength walked up to the tense child.

Strength:

Kindness, is everything alright?

Kindness:

Of course. Why?

Strength:

It's just…hey! Were those stairs here this whole time?

Narrator:

They noticed a staircase paved along the side of the mountain.

They shrugged at each other and journeyed down the stairs back to Hazelton.

Kindness:

Where's Greed?

Strength:

He went ahead. Is there something you need?

Kindness:

No…actually.

I must tell you something,

Something I've known for weeks.

Narrator:

Brave walked happily down the stairs ahead of his brothers,

While Kindness and Strength whispered to each other.

Kindness:

We each have titles and duties for Hazelton.

But Brave? None.

Strength:

What are you saying?

Kindness:

The Handsome Greed for financial aid,

Maths, science, the smartest brain.

The Mighty Strength to help the weak.

The Beloved Kindness for mental relief.

Yet Brave, he has no title. He has no duties.

He tries to help our people at least.

Strength:

What are you thinkin'?

Kindness:

That Love and Creed made us for a reason.

We each have titles; we each have a name.

It wouldn't be like them to disregard Brave.

Strength:

So why did they?

They shouldn't!

Kindness:

They didn't.

During the contest Brave and I snuck into the temple.

Strength:

Our parent's temple!

You know that's forbidden!

Kindness:

And I know we were without permission.

I also know we weren't the first to enter it.

In that temple I found their will.

The one they wrote, not the one that kills.

Why would they encourage us to fight,

When they've always told us to do what's right?

And that robe that Greed carries around,

It doesn't belong to him, and neither the crown.

We saw the crown in the temple,

It fits Brave perfectly, from temple to temple.

…It's like it was made for him.

Our parents are orderly, they never mishap.

They wanted a king and never this trap.

And in their will, what they have written,

Is for the one with no title to be King of Hazelton.

That is his title, it belongs to Brave.

Someone stole what our parents gave.

And I have a feeling, by his sharp mind and grin.

Greed falsified their will for his own skin.

He broke into the temple first,

He stole the robe and made this curse.

He wrote a will and placed it for the pope,

And soon to be king, he did hope.

He figured the people would vote for him.

He believed he would win.

And when I won, he became furious.

I only backed down because I knew the truth.

And when things started to get serious,

I hid it from Brave, I hid it from you.

It wasn't kind of me to break the rules.

It wasn't kind of me to keep a secret.

I didn't know what to do.

Out of fear for myself, I did keep it.

I'm afraid of Greed and even more now.

And to approach him with news, I don't know how.

He promised a cure for my wife,

So, confronting him would cost her life.

You knew our parents better than I.

So, you know that trip seemed awry.

And you've said it yourself, "What our parents say goes."

Green beeth the grass, red beeth the rose.

Winter bringeth spring.

Brave beeth the king.

I didn't take that potion but not because I didn't want to,

I didn't take that potion because I wasn't supposed to.

Strength:

If you had spoken sooner, we wouldn't have taken that route!

Kindness:

But in the end, it all worked out.

Brave…is…king.

Strength:

And you're as filthy as Greed.

Narrator:

They made it to the bottom of the staircase.

Willa appeared to congratulate.

Willa:

Wasn't that just wonderful, Brave!

O, the look on your face.

Well, that was one long journey. And I won't make you go through it again.

Narrator:

Willa spun her hands and made a portal for the brothers to walk in.

Willa:

Good luck boys and King of Hazleton.

O, and Slayer of Zaguah the Dragon!

Narrator:

Willa giggled and waved as the brothers walked through.

And home within seconds were The Promising Few.

Scene **V**. Hazelton

Narrator:

The brothers walked into Hazelton. The sky went from pale to sunny.

The citizens noticed their entrance and began running.

They cheered for the brothers returning safe from their journey.

The pope approached them with a smile and glee.

Pope:

Who, who is our king?

Strength:

Brave. *Brave is King.*

Pope:

Brave?

Man 1:

Was this a mistake?

Strength:

No. It was meant to be.

Narrator:

Running towards Kindness was his son Pete.

Priscilla followed him. They stopped at his feet.

Priscilla and Pete:

Daddy! Daddy!

Kindness:

Priscilla! Pete!

How is mommy?

Pete:

She's…asleep.

Kindness:

Well, let's go see.

Pope:

Strength, how could this be?

Strength:

I know how uncertain this seems.

But Brave has been amazing.

You weren't there to see the things

He's done. He deserves to be king.

Brave:

Yea, and I slain the mighty Zaguah dragon!

Man 1:

I find that hard to imagine.

Strength:

Well, he did it! And you shall respect him as so!

Brave is your newfound king whether you like it or don't.

We will not stand here and listen to you whine and moan.

Pope:

The people are just worried about their future that he holds.

He is in charge of five thousand souls.

But of course, we shall have a celebration.

Tomorrow we will hold his coronation.

And we thank him,

'King Brave of Hazleton, Slayer of Zaguah the Dragon'.

Narrator:

Kindness runs from his home crying with his wife in his arms.

Her body was grey and covered with scars.

Kindness:

Strength! Greed!

Where is Greed?

My wife! She's dying!

Strength:

Greed…

He left…to another city.

Kindness:

He promised me!

He promised a cure.

My wife, she's...look at her!

Narrator:

Kindness sat down with his wife on the ground.

The pope grabbed her wrist, but no pulse was found.

Pope:

Kindness, I'm afraid-

I'm-

Kindness:

No! Don't you say it. We still have time.

She can be saved!

Greed can make something to bring her to life!

Strength:

Kindness, this- this is unfortunate.

But there is nothing we can do about it.

Greed cannot conjure up the dead.

Kindness:

But Nevar can!

Or Willa! One of them can revive her!

Pope:

Reviving the dead is debarred!

Kindness:

Your God did it!

He, Jesus!

Pope:

You shall spend no more time with those witches!

God forbids!

It is a sin!

Kindness:

So, mom and dad can turn to witches.

But if I do it, God forbids it?!

My wife was alone while I was on a mission.

And none of you thought of paying her a visit!?

Woman 1:

Even if we did, what could we have done?

Greed took his medicine and left us with none.

Kindness:

You're questioning!

Strength:

And so art thee.

Kindness:

I knew I shouldn't have left. I'm sorry…

I'm sorry.

Narrator:

Kindness cried and held his wife tight.

Snot dripped from his nose; tears flooded his eyes.

Clouds came and covered the sun and sky.

His children sobbed from hearing his cries.

No one has ever seen Kindness so depressed.

It was the first time his feelings had been expressed.

The citizens watched him hold his wife to his chest.

He kissed her lips and caressed her breasts.

Brave:

Kindness, my coronation is tomorrow.

And right after we can have her funeral.

We will place her next to dad and mom,

Under the Tree of Palm.

It's the least I can do for you.

Kindness:

Thank you.

Narrator:

Kindness carried his wife back to his home.

The citizens continued their day and groaned.

They mourned and Kindness' children whimpered.

Strength:

Damn you, Greed.

Narrator:

Strength whispered.

Brave sat near the Lake of Love

Washing his daggers of blood.

He smiled and grinned ear to ear.

But something was in the atmosphere.

He had a feeling that something was near.

The sun kept peeking through the clouds.

The wind kept making strange sounds.

Brave looked around,

For nothing to be found.

He squinted his eyes and looked up at the sun.

He ignored it once more. Then he was done

Cleaning his daggers. The sun shined brightly.

The brightness was strange and frightening.

Brave looked down at his daggers, the rubies and pearls were blinking.

Brave's hands shook and he began thinking.

Brave held his daggers up to the sun and lined up the pearls.

He looked into the white pearls and the wind whirled.

He put down his daggers in disbelief.

He rose them once more and he did see,

The next historic calamity.

He rose from the ground and stood on his feet.

The rubies were still glistening.

He ripped open his shirt and exposed his chest.

He placed the rubies on his left breast.

His heart was beating loud and quick.

He sweated, panted, and became sick.

He ran into the city of Hazelton,

In search of his brothers, Kindness and Strength.

Brave:

Strength! Kindness!

Look at this!

Strength:

What is it, Brave? What happened?

Brave:

My daggers! I held the pearls up to the sun.

I saw fire and rocks. Those things will come.

Then I held the rubies to my heart, and it started rushing.

It felt like my blood was gushing.

Strength:

What does that mean?

Kindness:

Holding the pearls to the sun will tell you what's coming.

Holding the rubies to his heart means…start running.

Strength:

What exactly did you see?

Brave:

It was red like fire, it was falling!

Kindness:

The witch's prophecy.

She said she saw brown and red for the king and his city.

She said there would be heat, grey, and fires of clay, all coming.

Brave:

Fires of clay. What does that mean?

And it will be falling?

Narrator:

Strength looked out the window of his post.

His face turned as pale as a ghost.

He heard a loud rumbling noise.

Strength:

Asteroids…

And Greed was smart to avoid

Coming back.

Sly and black,

He is.

Kindness:

So, this is it?

The next calamity in history.

That just means…

The end of Hazelton's time?

Brave:

We're going to die!

Strength:

Calm down, Brave.

We need to evacuate.

Kindness:

I have to find my children!

Strength:

Brave, make sure everyone leaves all buildin's.

We'll go our way to The City of Hahm.

Brave:

But I'm, I'm, I'm, I'm…

Strength:

Brave, stay calm.

Narrator:

The brothers rushed out of Strength's station.

With bass, Strength hollered for the city's attention.

Strength:

CITY OF HAZELTON! LISTEN TO ME!! A TERRIBLE SHOWER IS HERE TO COME!

EVACUATE THROUGH THE FRUITFUL FOREST AND MAKE YOUR WAY TO THE CITY OF HAHM!!

DO NOT BOTHER PACKING YOUR THINGS!

GRAB YOUR CHILDREN AND QUICKLY LEAVE!

Narrator:

The confused citizens began to scurry.

They screamed, cried, and ran in a hurry.

An asteroid fell onto the Forbidden Temple.

The horses jumped out of control.

The beautiful temple had fallen and shattered.

The fragments flew and the horses scattered.

Kindness helped his children onto the pope's carriage.

His wife was packed along with his baggage.

Pope:

Kindness, wait. What are you doing with her?

Kindness:

My wife may be dead, but she deserves a funeral.

I am not leaving her in this town to burn.

Narrator:

Kindness placed her corpse in the pope's gig.

He loaded their bags and kissed his kids.

Priscilla:

But daddy, you're not coming with?

Kindness:

No, I have a city I need to assist.

Priscilla:

I don't want you to go.

Kindness:

I know.

But I took an oath.

There's no need to cry.

Pete will take care of you, right?

Pete:

I- I can try.

But you'll die.

Kindness:

No. This isn't goodbye.

Narrator:

The pope rode off with Priscilla and Pete.

A woman had fallen, he helped her on her feet.

Woman 1:

Thank you, Kindness. I'm feeling weak.

Kindness:

You'll be fine, no need to worry.

Narrator:

Kindness helped the woman onto a wagon.

He looked around his city in agon'.

Kindness:

Citizens! Board a wagon of a Bobbie or Peeler!

Lady Salas:

What about the people in the Dungeon of Dealers!

Strength:

We cannot save everyone here!

Lady Salas:

My husband is there!

Strength:

We're well aware!

Kindness:

Don't worry madam,

I'll go get him!

Strength:

You will not save him; it will cost you your life!

Kindness:

That is not for you to decide!

Narrator:

The pope returned with Kindness' children,

Loads of citizens had followed him.

Pope:

Strength! A disaster has happened!

The trees of the Fruitful Forest have fallen.

There is no way through, no way past them!

The only way out is through those mountains!

Narrator:

As asteroids fell and ended most citizens.

The brothers pondered ways to escape Hazelton.

Fiery balls flew and landed.

Strength held up his arm and he demanded.

Strength:

HAZELTON!

RETREAT TO THE MOUNTAINS!

Narrator:

He pointed and the citizens followed his directions.

But Strength's voice was far too powerful.

The grounds of the city started to rumble.

They looked towards the blue mountains.

A rockslide was caused by The Mighty Strength.

Rocks fell and rolled towards Hazelton.

Scared and despaired were the citizens.

With nowhere to go, they all scrambled

Like wild chickens. They then were trampled

By horses and carriages. The city was dismantled.

These natural disasters were too much to handle.

Brave did his best to help his people.

He tried to save them from the bound evil.

He looked up at the sky and saw an owl.

It passed him by. It seemed to have smiled.

He held his daggers up, but there was no sun.

No moon to tell him what to do.

He looked into the rubies and saw a red void.

He put them down and saw an asteroid.

Before he could run or even speak.

The asteroid landed at his feet.

His entire body started to bleed.

All he could do was anxiously scream.

Strength ran his way and grabbed the asteroid.

It burned his hands, but he tried to avoid

The pain he felt, so his brother, he could save.

He removed the asteroid. But dead was Brave.

His body was burnt and covered in blood.

His body was moulded into the mud.

His daggers in hands, his eyes wide open,

His mouth as well. His jaw was broken.

Strength:

Brave.

Narrator:

He cried while tears fell down his face.

He waited for an answer

From his dead brother.

Another asteroid had fallen.

It toppled a wagon

Holding Kindness' children.

Strength went over to assist the pope.

The children were fine but there was no hope

For the pope.

Pope:

I fear this is my time. There is no escape from this disaster.

The city is blocked at every entrance and destroyed along the pasture.

There is nothing I or my God can do.

This may be up to you, the strongest Few.

Narrator:

The pope closed his eyes as blood dripped from his mouth.

He said his final words and then died.

Strength grabbed Kindness' kids and pulled them out.

With few injuries, they both cried.

Strength:

Don't worry, loves. Have you seen your dad?

Pete:

He went towards the fire, to save Sir Salas.

Narrator:

Strength looked towards the temple that had collapsed.

The temple and its surroundings were completely crushed.

Strength mounted a wild brown horse.

He ran through the field that once was green.

The horse jumped and dodged the asteroids.

As horrific as it sounded, it was a beautiful scene.

The fire was ombre in purple and red.

When they hit the ground it shined orange and yellow.

The fragments flew and scratched Strength's head.

The rocks were like fireworks bursting. The cello

Was the sound of these falling rocks.

They made music along with the horse's trots.

Strength frowned as he made his way towards Kindness.

The sky was golden; the air was of dryness.

The sun peeked out and reflected off his golden hair.

He ripped off his purple skirt and waved it in the air.

He found his baby brother with arrows sticking out of his chest.

He dismounted his horse and placed his hands on Kindness' breasts.

Kindness' white suit was dyed red.

Strength wrapped his skirt around Kindness' head.

Strength:

Kindness! Kindness!

I thought I told you not to worry about Salas.

Why didn't you listen to me! How dare you disobey!?

Salas is a useless lame. Not worth to save.

Kindness:

We- We are 'The Promising Few of Hazelton'. We help the p-poor and protect the…lame.

Narrator:

Kindness smiled at his brother.

Whom he saw in different colours.

Strength laughed as well

As more asteroids fell.

Strength:

We protect the disabled lame.

Not that walking shame.

You're just…you're too kind.

You've lost your mind.

Kindness:

Maybe. But I– did what's right.

Narrator:

Kindness then mourned in desperate pain.

Strength held his hand as Kindness spoke profane.

Kindness:

It hurts…everywhere, it.

Strength:

Can you move, Kindness?

Kindness. Wh-what happened?

Kindness:

I don't think you'd believe it.

A man with precision,

Missed his target,

And his arrows returned to him,

Aimed for his heart. I missed it.

Strength:

What were you aiming at that you missed?

Kindness:

An asteroid, Strength.

Strength:

You tried to shoot down an asteroid! You bloke!

Kindness:

It was a joke.

Narrator:

Kindness weakly laughed.

Strength:

Do not play me like that.

But what happened?

Kindness:

It just…landed.

I flew over and…

Ehhh.

But no more me…my children?

Strength:

Your kids are safe.

Kindness:

And Brave?

Strength:

Him, I could not save.

Narrator:

Kindness looked away.

Kindness:

Just make sure…that my children are okay.

Okay?

Strength:

Okay.

Kindness:

Okay…

Can you…please…

Promise me…

Promise me that my wife will have a funeral?

Strength:

I promise. And I promise it will be beautiful.

Kindness:

She likes cherry blossoms. Plant a tree at her headstone. Will you do that?

Strength:

I will make sure she has what you asked.

Kindness:

In my pocket, it's our parents' will.

Narrator:

Strength palmed the letter and got a chill.

Kindness:

I'm sorry I lied to you.

Strength:

I love you.

Kindness:

I love…you.

Narrator:

Kindness smiled as he passed away.

Strength kissed his lips.

He mounted his horse and went his way

To check on Kindness' kids.

Several asteroids fell onto Hazelton.

Strength could not save his citizens.

The asteroids showered down like a rainstorm.

The city was bloody and warm.

Strength jumped off his horse and onto Kindness' kids.

He guarded their lives while risking his.

The final asteroids fell on top of Strength.

They were piled and stacked on top of him.

The city was strangely silent.

The citizens that survived gathered around.

Priscilla and Pete were nowhere to be found.

The citizens stared at the pile of asteroids sitting in the middle of the city.

After believing Strength and the kids were gone, the pile started shaking.

Out from the pile was The Mighty Strength holding the asteroids to the sky.

The few citizens left cheered and screamed, others wanted to cry.

Strength threw the asteroids off to the side and helped the kids out of the hole.

Their faces were dirty, but they were alive. They were choking on the brown smoke.

After standing silently in disarray, they suddenly heard a horse's neigh.

They looked towards the crumbled mountains to see a saviour coming their way.

The sun blocked them from seeing his features, but they could see black was he and his horse.

The saviour had a shiny black shield that paired with his long, silver, shimmering sword.

The saviour made his way to Hazelton.

As the smoke dispersed, they saw his sly grin.

He dismounted his horse. It was indeed,

No other than The Handsome Greed.

Greed:

Hazelton! HAHAHA! Look at thee!

In such desperate need!

In need of a king,

A king with prosperity.

O Strength, I knew you'd survive. Actually, I didn't.

I thought the other two would drag you down with them.

Strength:

Brave is dead.

Greed:

As destined.

Strength:

Kindness died.

Greed:

As did his wife.

Narrator:

The brothers began arguing with each other.

They swore, cursed, and talked over one another.

Strength:

You knew this would happen, you crooked, slimy, deceitful ass!

Greed:

Don't you dare speak to me like that!

Strength:

You promised Kindness' wife a cure.

Greed:

She was dead before we started our mission, that whore!

None of this would happen if I were voted king.

Strength:

You left Brave, Kindness, this city, and me!

You never cared about anyone or anything,

Just your stolen money!

Greed:

I knew you were dumb, but I didn't know you matched Brave.

I gave you a hint, Strength. You didn't take it! That was your mistake.

Strength:

Brave…Brave was meant to be king.

And Kindness, he told me.

You're a cheat.

Greed:

Kindness doesn't know what happened.

Strength:

I found this in his pockets.

Our parents' will.

The one they wrote, not the one that kills.

Greed:

It doesn't matter.

It's over.

Narrator:

Greed turned to what was left of the city.

He made a proposition for them to agree.

Greed:

Hazelton,

I hope you've come to the realisation

That I should have been chosen.

You are in need of food, money, and shelter,

Things that could not be provided by my brother.

Hazelton, you need to look no further.

If you agree with me being your ruler,

Simply raise your hand.

Narrator:

The citizens seemed to be hesitant.

But they realised that Greed was their last hope.

They each slowly raised their hands.

Greed smiled and adjusted his robe.

Strength:

The witch's spell: *no other shall be named King of Hazelton.*

Even if they voted you as king now, you couldn't.

Greed:

Look around you, there is no more Hazelton.

Once we are done repairing this poor setting.

I will name it…August City.

And I will be the very first king.

www.ingramcontent.com/pod-product-compliance
Lightning Source LLC
LaVergne TN
LVHW041736060526
838201LV00046B/831